The Gospel Isn't (Just) About Me Surrendering My Kingdom to Him

Dan Palmer & Cortney Alexander

The Gospel Isn't (Just) About Me: Surrendering My Kingdom to Him

Printed in the United States of America.

ISBN-13: 978-0692824580

Acknowledgements

Dan: I would like to start by thanking my Lord and Savior—You make all things possible. This project would never have started without the support of my biggest fan and greatest support, my beautiful and amazing wife of 22 years. Thank you for your sacrifice and love! I must also give a shout out to my nine children who inspire me every day to be the very best. You all are my favorite people in the world. Dad and mom, if it was not for your determination to dream bigger, I would never have been the dreamer I am today. When most said to me that I couldn't and I wouldn't be able to achieve, you always whispered in my ear, "You are and you will." Thank you! To all those who helped put this project together, we did it! Thank you!

Cortney: I owe my work in this book to two people in particular: First, Gary Bates of Creation Ministries International, who told me that I could believe the Bible means what it says. Second, my wife Claire, who prayed for me (and anointed me in my sleep) when I still wasn't sure I wanted the Bible to mean what it says. Thank you.

Contents

I.   Vain Conversation

There's a famous song called, "You're So Vain."[1] It's about a self-centered man whose vanity is so great that the singer says he'll probably even believe she's singing about him. In the decades since the song came out, several well-known men have publicly claimed that the song was about them. These men eagerly believed they were the subject of the song, even though it painted them in an unflattering light.

I can relate to those guys. I used to be so vain—so vain that I thought the gospel was about me. In that time of my life, I thought I was a Christian, but I was really living a vain conversation. That conversation would have ended in death—eternal death. But God redeemed me from that vain conversation. I'm going to tell you how.

A.   A Vain Conversation Usually Starts with a Partial Conversation

I'm going to explain what it means to be in a vain conversation. But first I'm going to tell you how someone ends up in a vain conversation. It starts with a partial conversation. You're probably asking, "What's a partial conversation?" Let's start with an example.

Picture yourself driving in your car on a Sunday night. You're listening to the radio (Christian radio, of course). When it comes to a commercial break, you're not interested in the advertisement for the upcoming Kari Jobe concert— you've already bought your tickets. So you tune in to a talk-news station. But you weren't prepared for what happens next.

The program is suddenly interrupted with breaking news. A meteor just slammed into a nearby town, killing a large

---

[1] Carly Simon. "You're So Vain." *No Secrets*, Elektra, 1972.

1

number of people. Not long after, a new report comes in that the meteor wasn't actually a meteor—it was a metal cylinder. A few minutes later, you learn that the metal cylinder has opened, and living beings have emerged. And they don't look friendly.

The Secretary of the Interior comes on the radio broadcast, urging people to remain calm. But it isn't working. People are rushing into the streets, looking up to see what will come out of the sky next. You try to call 911, but the lines are jammed. People rush into churches, turning the Sunday-night service into an "end-of-the-world" prayer meeting. And other people start looking for their guns.

All this really happened on October 30, 1938. Fortunately, no one was seriously hurt as people were running to and fro—even the people struck by the cylinder. Because there was no cylinder and no aliens; it was just a radio drama. The fictional nature of the program was announced at the outset, then three more times during the program. Yet thousands of people missed that critical piece of information and were thrown into panic by these events.

The radio listeners jumped to a wrong conclusion based on a partial conversation. A partial conversation occurs when we overhear part of a conversation, then jump to conclusions without ever learning the whole conversation. Instead, we combine the facts we've heard with our own assumptions to fill in the missing pieces with our own assumptions. But our assumptions are often wrong.

I'm not suggesting that we always carry on partial conversations with bad intent. But even when we enter a partial conversation innocently, it can lead us to a wrong conclusion. Here's another example from my own life.

I was coaching my first game as a seventh-grade basketball

coach. It was the fourth quarter and we were up by a few points against a team greater in height by an average of six inches. This team crushed our team year after year. I grew more anxious as the clock ticked off the last seconds. Then, a referee called a foul on us. Like every good coach, I raised my voice to grab the referee's attention in hope that he would approach me to hear my concerns. Respectfully, I explained my position and asked him what he thought of my opinion. The next thing I knew, the other referee came over to the scoring table and called a technical foul because the jersey number of one of my players was different than that listed on the official team roster. The other team capitalized on the technical to win the game by one point.

Afterward, I encouraged the boys, then sat down by my wife, hoping to receive some encouragement myself. Smiling, she said, "Too bad you got a technical! What did you say to the referee?" As I explained that the technical was for the jersey number, not what I said, it hit me that the families and fans probably thought the same thing. Based on the facts they observed, they would logically conclude that something I said to the referee prompted the technical, and therefore that I cost us the game.

They came to a logical conclusion based on solid facts. Yet they still lacked truth because they did not know the whole story. What if they had acted on their wrong conclusion? They might have fired the coach. But that would have been futile. Not only would they have lost a great coach, it also wouldn't have solved the problem. They needed to fire the dad in charge of the roster! But without the full story, they would have made the wrong decision.

In these examples, no one died as a result of the partial conversation. But it does happen. In the book of Hosea, God says, "My people are destroyed for lack of knowledge." Hosea 4:6. God's people didn't lack knowledge because they lacked access to knowledge. God has always made knowledge available to those who listen—He says in Isaiah, "Do you not know? Do you not hear? Has it not been told you from the beginning . . . from the foundations of the earth?" Isaiah 40:21-23. God's people lacked knowledge because they "rejected knowledge." Hosea 4:6. I don't think this word was just for Hosea's day—I believe it still happens every day. Let's look at why that is.

1.   People pay attention to facts that appeal to them

We pay attention to facts that appeal to us—especially facts that are about us.

In the alien-invasion example, people panicked because they thought *they* were threatened. We can probably relate to them—when we receive information that we're in danger, we don't usually hang around waiting to make sure we get the whole story. We react immediately.

But it's not just danger that grabs our attention. We pay attention to facts that appeal to us. In other words, we listen to what we like to hear. We eat what we like to taste. We look at what is pleasant to our eyes.

Lots of times, this isn't a big deal. Here's an example: I bet you're not that excited about looking at pictures of other people's kids or vacations. But you do like looking at pictures of your own. Your attention is drawn to what most interests you. And we are really interested in things about *us* and things that *benefit* us or threaten to *harm* us. We pay attention to those.

The problem arises when this tendency causes us to overlook the things that don't so obviously benefit us—because sometimes missing those facts causes us to miss the truth. We settle for a partial conversation, rather than making the effort to learn the whole conversation.

Let me give you an example of partial conversation on a national scale. As of mid-2016, the United States owes a national debt of approximately $19.3 Trillion, a number rising at a fast pace. While opinions differ on just how big of a problem this is, I don't think any American likes his country owing that much money. So why doesn't the government take greater measures to rein in the expanding debt? In part, the government fails to act because the people who elect congressmen and presidents—American citizens—are engaged in a partial conversation about this issue.

American citizens, whether Republican or Democrat, tend to have ears finely tuned to facts about how government spending or taxes will affect their short-term interests. Since any plan to reduce the national debt will involve lower government spending and/or higher taxes, it will get a lot of attention—and much of it not positive. On the other hand, few people have ears to hear predictions about the long-term dangers of our national debt—they are too easy to ignore because they don't carry an immediate effect. The result: many of our elected officials, both Republican and Democrat, spend a lot more time addressing their respective constituency's short-term priorities instead of the long-term (unappealing) problem of the national debt.

The first partial conversation in history occurs in Genesis 3. God told Adam not to eat of the fruit of the Tree of Knowledge of Good and Evil, or he would surely die. Genesis 2:17. But then the serpent comes along and hooks Eve into a conversation about the forbidden fruit.

The topic of the fruit interested her enough to engage the serpent in conversation, but what he said next must have been music to her ears. After Eve recited God's warning not to eat the fruit lest you die, the serpent responded, "You will not surely die. For God knows that in the day you eat of it your eyes will be opened, and *you will be like God.*" Genesis

3:22.

The serpent's words appealed to Eve—and they prompted her to action. Scripture says that "when the woman saw that the tree was good for food, that it was pleasant to the eyes, and a tree desirable to make one wise, she took of its fruit and ate." Genesis 3:6. Eve heard that the fruit could make her like God, and she was sucked in. She ate. And not just her, but Adam too.

We all know what happened next. One of the consequences of their sin was that God pulled them away from the Tree of Life, lest they eat and live forever. Genesis 3:22-23. As God promised, they surely died.

Eve's story illustrates that a partial conversation can still involve some true facts. The serpent spoke a fact when he said Adam and Eve would become like God. I say this because, after they ate, God said, "Behold, the man has become like one of Us, to know good and evil." Genesis 3:22-23. But Eve surely did not understand what that would entail—she operated from a flawed understanding. And she failed to go back to her Creator, who could give her the proper perspective and bring her into the whole conversation. Eve acted based only on the facts that appealed to her, leading her to jump to a wrong conclusion based on the limited facts she knew.

Here is a critical point: The enemy of God knows he cannot convince most people that God does not exist— creation itself witnesses to us that there is a God. Romans 1:18-21; Psalm 19:1-4. Adam and Eve didn't deny God's existence. And Satan didn't try to make them. In fact, his first words to Eve acknowledged God's existence: "Has God indeed said?" Yet Satan led Adam and Eve into death through a conversation that started with the topic of God's word. If Satan cannot get us to outright deny God's existence, the next best thing is to keep us from the fullness of the Truth. He doesn't want us to join God in the whole conversation about the kingdom of heaven.

2. Facts versus truth

Before we go further, we need to understand the difference between facts and truth. Facts provide knowledge, but not necessarily truth. When Adam and Eve ate of the tree, they demonstrated an appetite for facts. But loving facts does not equal loving truth. This is a problem, since God is Truth.

Here are a few examples demonstrating that facts do not equal truth:

Fact	Truth
One plus one equals **two**.	One plus one equals **one** . . . in marriage. Mark 10:6-8.

If you enter into marriage living by the fact that one plus one equals two, you will fight for your rights, position, and your dreams in the marriage. If you believe the truth, that one plus one equals one, you will then lay down your rights, position, and dreams for that truth. The husband and wife will lose their life to become one. The word says that two fleshes become **one**.

Fact	Truth
If you lose your life, you will not have a life.	Jesus said we must lose our life in order to find it. Matthew 10:39.

Believing the fact causes a person to hold onto his life and partner only with those who will help preserve him. He will make decisions that build security of life, such as wealth. But when someone lives by the truth, he does not make decisions based on how to survive. He makes decisions on how to live dead. He does not live for himself, but for love, which is selfless.

Fact	Truth
What you sow, you will reap.	Mercy! Jesus Christ!

It's a fact that a farmer will reap what he sows. If he plants wheat seed, he will reap a harvest of wheat. It's also a fact that every man and woman since Adam has sown a life of the sin, and that we deserve to reap eternal death. Yet it's truth that Jesus Christ laid down His life (and took it up again) so that God might show mercy: instead of eternal death, we may reap eternal life through Christ.

These examples demonstrate that facts, in isolation, do not always lead to truth. Worse, partial conversations typically lead us to complete error.

3. Knowledge puffs you up; Truth brings you to your knees

While our appetite for facts often leads us into partial

conversations, we have to overcome this tendency. Because engaging in a partial conversation not only leads us into error, it can also give a false confidence, hardening us against the truth. Fact without truth is knowledge without God. The intellectual knowledge empowers us, causing us to feel like a god.

Scripture warns against knowledge that is not driven by love for God. It puffs us up. It makes us prideful. Have you ever met a person who knows the craziest facts and wants to make sure that you know that they know these facts? Does he want to share them because he wants to educate you or because he wants to make himself sound smart?

Many people even preach facts without preaching truth. I sometimes wrote sermons that contained Scripture, but they didn't capture the truth of Scripture. Other times, I spoke truth that the Lord said to me, without *being* the truth He spoke. I was like Balaam's donkey. The donkey spoke truth, but did not understand it himself. That was me.

Are you asking yourself, "What is he talking about?" Let me give an illustration. In America, our criminal justice system is designed to seek the truth. We don't want to convict an innocent man. In seeking the truth, we allow witnesses to testify about the relevant facts. But, generally, we don't let a witness testify about what someone else told him. We require that the witness testify only about his personal knowledge. What he has seen with his eyes and heard with his ears.

In the greatest sermon, the "sermon on the Mount," Jesus did not try to come up with something to preach. Instead, He spoke about the life He walked out. His sermon was about who He was. Jesus did not prepare a sermon; He was the sermon. So the Truth of what we preach must be within us.

Many go out and witness what they know (factually) about God. To go and witness is different than being a witness. Jesus did not say, "go and witness," He said, "go and *be* a witness." Acts 1:8. Scripture gives us an example of the distinction in Acts 19. It says, "God was doing extraordinary miracles by the hands of Paul." Acts 19:11. This didn't go unnoticed. People were even carrying handkerchiefs that Paul had touched to sick people—and then diseases and evil spirits left them. Acts 19:12. Paul was a witness.

When Paul preached the gospel, he wasn't just preaching what someone had told him. He was preaching what he experienced. Paul had seen God do extraordinary miracles by his hand, enabling him to write to the Corinthians that their "faith should not be in the wisdom of men but in the power of God." 1 Corinthians 2:4. Because "the kingdom of God is not in word but in power." 1 Corinthians 4:20. Paul wasn't just witnessing *about* what someone told him regarding the kingdom of God. Paul was a witness *to* the kingdom of God. So he was able to be a witness about the kingdom of God.

You might be saying, "How am I supposed to compete with that? Nobody's seeing miracles through handkerchiefs I've touched!" Don't give up on the miracles! "Earnestly desire the spiritual gifts, especially that you may prophesy." 1 Corinthians 14:1 (ESV). In the meantime, you don't have to compete with Paul or anyone else to be a witness. If you are born again, you are a witness to the power of God.

Why do I say that all born-again believers have witnessed the power of God? If we are in Christ, then we know that we were once slaves to the sin, and have now been set free! Romans 6:17-18. We each are a testimony of what God has done in our lives. We are a witness to that. Consider the words of the blind man healed by Jesus. When the Jewish authorities were questioning him about who healed him, accusing Jesus of being a sinner, the man simply gave his testimony: "Whether He is a sinner or not I do not know. One thing I know: that though I was blind, now I see." John 9:25.

When we are a witness to what God has done in our lives, it will usually make a stronger impact on an unbeliever than hitting him with a barrage of Bible knowledge. Look at the blind man: His testimony had such an impact that the Jewish leaders cast him out of the synagogue! John 9:34. That might not be the result you're hoping for when you share your testimony, but read what happened next: "When Jesus heard what had happened, he found the man." John 9:35 (NLT). If you stick with Jesus, the world may cast you out, but He will find you!

On the other hand, Acts 19 gives us an example of those who try to live by knowledge without having truth. Right after we read about the miracles God performed through Paul, this chapter tells us that seven sons of a Jewish high priest named Sceva attempted to cast out evil spirits by saying, "I adjure you by the Jesus whom Paul proclaims." Acts 19:13. Notice that Sceva's sons didn't invoke "Jesus, my Lord and my God." Instead, they tried to invoke "the Jesus whom Paul proclaims." They didn't know Jesus, they merely knew *of* Jesus. They were relying on secondhand facts, without knowing the truth themselves.

In short, this didn't work out well for them. An evil spirit was not impressed by their effort, answering, "Jesus I know, and Paul I recognize, but who are you?" Acts 19:15. Then, the possessed man "leaped on them, mastered all of them and overpowered them, so that they fled out of that house naked and wounded." Acts 19:16. These guys learned a valuable lesson that we all need to understand. It is only by having the truth in our hearts, rather than just in our heads, that we will be clothed by Jesus; otherwise, the shame of our nakedness will be revealed, just like the sons of Sceva. Revelation 3:15-

ple have a theology (that is, a belief system about ...) based in factual knowledge of Scripture instead of a deep relationship with God. To have a theology about faith is nothing like actually having faith. Jesus told the Jewish leaders, "You study the Scriptures diligently because you think that in them you have eternal life." John 5:39. That sounds good, right? After all, Paul commended Timothy because "from infancy you have known the Holy Scriptures, which are able to make you wise for salvation through faith in Christ Jesus." 1 Timothy 3:15 (NIV). So why did Jesus tell those Jewish leaders who searched the Scriptures so diligently, "You do not have His word abiding in you"? John 5:38.

Jesus said the Jewish leaders didn't have the word dwelling inside them because, even though they had memorized a lot of Scripture, they didn't let the Scripture impact their man-made theology. Look at what Jesus told another group of Jewish leaders: "You are mistaken, knowing neither the Scriptures nor the power of God." Matthew 22:29. They had memorized the Scripture, but they didn't *know* the Scripture. They entirely missed the point. Scripture tells us that faith is credited as righteousness. Romans 4:22-25. Yet the Jewish leaders gripped tightly to their theology of self-righteousness. Thinking they were already righteous, they "refuse[d] to come to [Jesus] to have life." John 5:40 (NIV).

Even though these religious leaders memorized the word, they couldn't see the Word (Jesus) right in front of them. Why? Because they didn't have "room in [their] hearts for [Jesus'] message." John 8:37 (NLT). They knew a lot of facts, but they had no room for facts that didn't fit their worldview, in which the glory they received from men was more important than the glory that comes from God. John 5:44.

Jesus' exchange with the Jewish leaders demonstrates that, while the Truth is full of facts, facts do not always equal truth. The many facts the religious leaders knew didn't lead them to the Truth. It's not that facts are bad, but we must resist the inclination to listen only to the facts we're comfortable with. We have to be willing to make room in our hearts for the Truth.

Once we have The Truth, we become truth, for He lives in us! Galatians 2:20. Therefore, in serving as a witness for Christ, we don't just tell people what we know, we tell people who we are.

Many believe in universal facts, but deny the existence of universal truths. This isn't new. The Roman governor Pontius Pilate rhetorically asked Jesus, "What is truth?" John 18:38. People do not want Truth because it requires responsibility. Facts only inform, without requiring responsibility. For example, merely having facts about abortion does not convey a responsibility to do anything, but an understanding the truth about abortion demands responsive action. In this age, knowledge is glorified, while holding fast to a particular truth is often seen as ignorance because you are not open to different interpretations of truth.

But what good are facts if they do not lead to The Truth? Facts without truth are generally useless—except for someone trying to deceive. A life of gaining facts without reaching The Truth leads to loneliness and an addiction to information. Paul talked about such people, saying they are "always learning and never able to come to a knowledge of the truth." 2 Timothy 3:7 (NKJV). This addiction came into mankind via the Tree of Knowledge of Good and Evil. The only way to break this addiction is to develop a hunger for The Truth. An appetite for The Truth will create an appetite for the Tree of Life. Revelation 2:7.

Why is it hard to develop an appetite for The Truth? It takes faith. Faith is required to overcome our addiction to facts. If we are driven solely by facts, we will always keep looking for more facts to prove the Truth. But, without faith, there will never be enough facts. Someone can be presented with all the amazing facts supporting the truth of the gospel, yet fail to be persuaded because his addiction to facts causes him to crave still more. Think of Pilate asking, "What is truth?" right after hearing The Truth. So we must not be driven by a love for facts, but by a love for The Truth. With God's grace, a love for truth will develop into a love for The Truth.

Often, someone who learns a lot about a subject ends up feeling even less informed because he now appreciates the vast amount of information that still exists beyond his comprehension. A few years ago, I met a doctor who specialized in breast cancer. She explained to me that her studies focused on one cell of the breast. I was in awe of all this doctor knew about this narrow area of medicine—she had spent thirteen years in labs studying this issue. I said, "You must be a master in this area." She smiled and replied, "I expect that in five years, what I currently know will be elementary in comparison to the groundbreaking information that will enhance the scientific field."

Thirteen years of school and lab work, followed by many years in the profession, and this lady was only able to gain temporary expertise about one tiny part of the body. There is so much more to know, not only in her field, but also in our entire body. How much more in the universe?

What an overwhelming concept! The more we learn, the more we realize how much we don't know. If we make our life about learning every fact, it will end in futility.

When we live on an appetite of facts, our paradigm is built

on information, but not necessarily truth. We collect facts about our past experiences, present situations, and our future fears. Usually, we apply a filter to accept only the facts we're comfortable with. Then, we develop a pattern of thinking that determines the way we see and hear the world.

In other words, many of us live a partial conversation. If we think we "know" based on our partial conversation, we probably won't seek out the whole truth.

Jesus wants us to be free from this deception and to have The Truth. This requires that we live life from His perspective instead of ours. This is why Jesus often said, "Those who have ears to hear, let them hear" and "those who have eyes to see, let them see." The love of knowledge blinds us from the love of the Father and the truth of the Gospel. When our eyes see and our ears hear, we are given the opportunity for our paradigm to shift. The Truth sets us free from the lie that results from a partial conversation.

In summary, partial conversations are tempting because they suck us in with facts that are pleasant to our ears. Yet, most often, they cause us to reach a false conclusion. As believers, we walk a road that travels from loving facts to falling in love with The Truth. Chasing facts requires zero faith; setting your heart on The Truth requires great faith. As believers, we need to be aware of the temptation and the trappings of entering a partial conversation in all areas of our lives, but especially our relationship with God.

B. A Partial Conversation Can Become a Vain Conversation

If we continue in a partial conversation with God (that is, we live according to only those facts that appeal to us without ever discovering Truth), our life can become a vain conversation.

1. A vain conversation doesn't produce fruit

What's a vain conversation? The word "vain" means useless or futile. If we do something in vain, it means that it won't be fruitful. So a vain conversation is one that doesn't produce fruit, like the tree Jesus cursed for failing to bear fruit.

Think back to the alien-invasion example—it's an example of a vain conversation. When people were running around in a panic because aliens had landed, they were reacting to a threat that didn't exist. And since the threat didn't exist, their reaction would accomplish nothing. It was in vain. It was futile.

And that's true of vain conversations generally. No matter how hard we try, no matter how good our intentions, nothing good will come of something done in vain. If we're operating from a fundamentally wrong assumption, it doesn't matter how long we work at it. It's futile. It won't produce good fruit. The vain conversation in the alien-invasion story turned out harmless, primarily because it didn't last long. But it doesn't always end so well. Vain conversation that goes unchecked can be a matter of life and death.

Let's go back to Eve's conversation with the serpent. Earlier, we called this a partial conversation because Eve had ears for facts that appealed to her. These limited facts led her to jump to a wrong conclusion because she wasn't considering the whole story. If we look closer, I think we'll see that Eve's conversation was not only partial—it was vain. The conversation was futile—it was not fruitful. Why do I say that? Look at the result of the conversation. God pulled them away from the Tree of Life, lest they eat and live forever. Genesis 3:22-23. As God had promised, they surely died. That's some bitter fruit.

2. One man's journey from vain conversation into the greater conversation

I once knew a young pastor who I could tell was on fire for the Lord. He was zeroed in on sermons. He was constantly reading the Bible, plus devotionals about the Bible. And he really got after it in worship. This was the kind of youth pastor you'd want for your kids. Have you ever known anyone like him?

But as time went on, I started to notice something about this young pastor. He listened to a lot of sermons, but tended to focus on a certain type of sermon. He read the Bible, but tended to focus on a certain type of passage. He read devotionals, but what was it about devotionals that attracted him? He was passionate in worship, but what was driving his passion?

There was a common theme to the sermons, Bible passages, and devotionals that drew his attention. They were all uplifting, feel-good messages. I also discovered why he loved worship so much. It made him feel really good.

You might ask how I knew so much about this young pastor. It was me. It took me quite a while to realize this about me—that I really only paid attention to the parts of the Bible, sermons, and worship services that made me feel good. I wasn't doing it intentionally. It's just what I was drawn to. Have you ever known anyone like me?

I began to recognize that I thought the Gospel was about

me. I was actually living a vain conversation. I was in love with facts about God that seemed (to me) in my best interest. I spent a lot of time doing Godly things, yet my focus in these activities was more on me than God.

Don't get me wrong. God was not out of my sight entirely; He was in my view. But He wasn't always my focus. For example, my prayer life revolved mostly around asking God to help, bless, and encourage me and those I cared about. I didn't take time to ask God what was on His heart— I always assumed I knew already. Since I was content with the facts I had about His interests, I focused on making sure He knew my interests and needs. I now recognize that my interests alone weren't the only pressing issues being addressed on the throne of God. But I didn't then. It made our relationship very one-sided.

When I did take the time to ask what interested God, I was only listening intently to the parts that would benefit or affect me. I do interest Him! But His interests are bigger than me. The funny thing is that while God already knew what interested me, I was pretty clueless about His interests unless it included me.

If you can sympathize with me, you might say, "Sure, you were in a partial conversation because you only paid attention to the facts that appealed to you. But why do you say your conversation with God was in vain?" Remember, a partial conversation, left unchecked, turns into a vain conversation. The story in the Bible about the young rich ruler is a good example of a vain conversation. He began a conversation with Jesus hoping that Jesus would come to his terms. He had done a lot of what Jesus asked, but was doing it for himself rather than the one He should have been doing it for. And that was where my conversation had ended up.

At that point, I was not simply clueless about God's

interests, I just wasn't that interested in His interests. I always wanted God to know my heart's desires, but I rarely (if ever) took the time to know His heart's desires. To the extent our interests overlapped, it was more coincidental than because I cared about His interests.

That's a problem. Picture a man and woman thinking about getting married. He says, "I really love you. I can't wait to share my life with you—to bring you into all my dreams for the future." The woman says, "Well, I'm glad you want me because I am desirable. I'm excited about what you'll share with me—I can always use more. Now about your dreams: I hope they're to my benefit, because I have a lot of my own dreams. Expensive dreams. I love the fact that you're really rich and can finance those expensive dreams. I would love to marry you!"

Would you say she really loved him? Would he go forward and seal that relationship? I don't think God would either. So my life was indeed a vain conversation. It was headed for futility.

When I became aware of my selfish heart, I began to realize that I preached to God's people all the parts of His Word that appealed to their self-interest. I shared truths with them without telling them the whole story. I spoke to their hearts' desire because I was not interested in His, unless it happened to benefit me and my audience. I was enticing people into the same vain conversation I was having with God.

3.   Is it just me?

As I have traveled the United States and the world, I find that my story is not unique. Many of us only listen to the conversations in the Scripture that we think are about us. According to Biblegateway.com, the most popular Bible verses are John 3:16, Jeremiah 29:11, and Romans 8:28. All these verses are amazing, but they have one thing in common if only read and understood as a single verse; they are easily interpreted to be merely about our benefit. These verses do capture God's desire for our rescue, His blessings on our life, and His good plans for us. As amazing as those truths are, if our main focus is ourselves we will easily miss the main point of those verses, as well as the whole Bible.

Even if we were to look at verses that reveal the character of God, we sometimes miss it if we're too near-sighted—that is, unable to see past our interest. Take John 3:16, for example: "For God so loved the world that He gave His only begotten Son, that whoever believes in Him should not perish but have everlasting life." What an awesome verse! But what do we focus on? Usually, we focus on the part that says, "should not perish but have everlasting life." Yes, that's amazing! But is that the most amazing part of the verse? Is the most amazing part of the verse where we read that God gave us His Son? Or His love for us?

What if all those parts, while absolutely breath taking, are still not the most amazing part ? How about the first part of the verse, which most read quickly without pondering: "For God." If that doesn't impact our hearts, then we are missing the true benefit of this verse. The essence of the benefit is not Jesus' death, but God Himself. This verse reveals Him. Without revelation of who He is, we cannot receive the fullness that He loves us because we do not know the One who loves us. If the words, "For God," do not stop us in our tracks and cause us to be in awe, then we are lacking the fullness of truth that this verse offers. This verse offers our most basic need (love), but we can only accept love in the measure we know who is loving us. The revelation of "For God" releases the full revelation of the meaning of His gift, His act, and His reward.

Romans 8:28 is another great example. It says, "And we know that all things work together for good to those who love God, to those who are the called according to His purpose." People often focus on the portion that says, "All things work together for good," but not so much the part about "to those who love God, to those who are the called according to His purpose." Why might that be? Could it be that the part about all things working for our good appeals to us more than the part about loving Him or being called according to His purpose, rather than *our* purpose? Paul highlights this idea when he writes out a prayer to the Ephesians, "That the God of our Lord Jesus Christ, the Father of glory, may give unto you the spirit of wisdom and revelation in the knowledge of him: The eyes of your understanding being enlightened; that ye may know what is the hope of his calling." Ephesians 1:17-18 (KJV). The key here is that we need the spirit of wisdom and revelation so that our eyes can see the whole conversation, which will open us to hope in God's calling (not our calling, but His calling).

Like a vain conversation, our focus on isolated Scriptures tends to mislead us. Let's look at one of the most popular verses and consider the context to see if we hear this verse applied correctly: "'For I know the plans that I have for you,' declares the LORD, 'plans for welfare and not for calamity, to give you a future and a hope.'" Jeremiah 29:11.

Most people read this verse and see blessings in their future. Most preach this verse in the same manner. Keep in mind that the poorest American on welfare is richer than 90% of the world. So we quote this Scripture seeking blessing upon blessings.

But the Israelites were not prospering when God gave them this promise. They were in captivity in Babylon. They would remain there for *70 years* because they had lived in sin and refused to repent, despite God's repeated pleas and warnings through the cries of the prophets.

God raised up the Babylonians to conquer the Israelites so that they would become poor in spirit and humble themselves before God. It worked. During their exile, they repented. In order to encourage them after they had repented, God gave them Jeremiah 29's promise of good plans and a hopeful future, letting them know they were not forgotten. He gave them this awesome Scripture to strengthen them to finish their term of captivity well, knowing they would have a great future.

Today, many people praying this verse for their lives do not understand its context. This verse is for those who, after walking away from God into the consequences of disobedience, have repented. This verse gives them hope in the midst of their (sometimes desperate) physical circumstances. While it doesn't promise that this current situation will disappear, it does promise a light at the end of the tunnel.

For example, say you are a woman who indulged in sex outside of marriage and got pregnant. And it turns out that when the guy said he loved you, he really just meant he loved himself. Now he's gone, leaving you to deal with the situation alone. What do you do?

If you're living a partial conversation, maybe the words of our abortion culture appeal to you: "It's legal. It's a woman's choice. Why should you sacrifice your life for a baby when you're not ready?" In a desperate situation, those words might sound good, but that path leads to a futile way of life— a vain conversation.

If you step out of partial conversation and into the greater conversation, Jeremiah 29:11 offers hope to you: "'I know the thoughts that I think toward you,' says the LORD, 'thoughts

of peace and not of evil, to give you a future and a hope.'"
That doesn't mean the road of single parenthood will be easy.
But it does mean that you have hope, and the hope is Him. If
you repent of the sin and seek Him, you will find Him—even
(maybe especially) in the midst of trouble. Understanding this
context opens our eyes to the whole truth of this verse.

4.   Jesus came to redeem us from vain conversation

What is the main purpose of the Bible? The reply is
consistent: "the redemption of man." That is what I was
taught in Bible college. And, yes, this is fact. Undoubtedly,
the rescue of man is one of Scripture's major themes. We see
God reaching into the world through friendship, laws,
covenants, prophecy, miracles, and even His coming in the
person of Jesus the Christ, to give us an opportunity to
receive His mercy, even unto salvation.

But is man's redemption the whole conversation? Is man's
salvation the centerpiece of the Scriptures? Before you
answer, let me ask a slightly different question: If *man's*
salvation is the centerpiece of Scripture, who is the subject of
the Bible? Man. Does that sound right to you?

Jesus died (and rose!) so we could escape vain
conversation. Almost two thousand years ago, the apostle
Peter encouraged believers that, "With the precious blood of
Christ," they had been redeemed from the "vain conversation
received by tradition from [their] fathers." 1 Peter 1:18-21
(KJV). Another translation says, "You were ransomed from
the futile ways inherited from your forefathers." 1 Peter 1:18
(ESV).

Does that verse have any applicability today? Have any of
us received any futile ways from our forefathers or the culture
that raised us? Have any of us sought after God for what
interests us, without taking much interest in what interests

Him? Have any of us allowed a partial conversation to become a vain conversation with God? If not us, how can we minister to those who have?

Let's take a step back and look at the entirety of the story. Let's see if we have been reading from the paradigm of a partial/vain conversation or the paradigm of The Truth. We'll start with the Gospel—the Good News.

II.   What is the Gospel?

A.   The Traditional Gospel

The Gospel is about man's salvation. Or is it?

Most of us read the Bible with the idea that the story begins at Genesis 1:1 and ends at Revelation 22:21. We read how God, through His Word, creates this amazing earth and everything in it. The story includes the creation of man and his fall; Noah and the flood; God's unconditional covenant with Abraham; and Moses and the ten commandments. Then comes our favorite part—Jesus Christ and His death and resurrection. Then we read about the church, with Jesus Christ returning on a great white horse, with hair as white as wool, eyes full of fire, a sword that proceeds from His mouth, and a name written on His thigh: King of kings and Lord of lords. He is coming soon!

These testimonies are amazing, both alone and in the greater context. We usually connect each of these stories to the theme of mankind's redemption. In keeping with this salvation-centered view of the Bible, most of our Sunday sermons are structured around salvation from our problems, finances, relationship, hopelessness, and sins.

I love the theme of salvation, especially redemption from sin. And I should love it because it came with a sacrifice that I will never fully comprehend. God sends His Son and sacrifices Him for a horrible sinner—me! That is so incredible and beautiful. But I wonder if I loved this redemptive theme, and have always thought this to be the Bible's central topic, because it involves my favorite topic—me!

So while the various flavors of salvation are indeed Biblical topics, we should question whether we focus so intently on them because *we* are the beneficiaries. As we read earlier, we tend to join conversations because we hear something that interests or benefits us. Could we be reading these stories through the lens of a partial conversation? Could that paradigm limit the truth we find in these great Biblical stories? Is there a greater conversation we are missing? And, if so, are there consequences for missing it?

When people play the lottery, they hope to be saved from their financial circumstances. They want financial security so that they will no longer worry about money, which they think will translate to a better life. But statistics show that 70% of lottery winners end up in bankruptcy just a few years later. While these winners thought they were saved from debts and other money problems, the "salvation" they found was only temporary. It turned out their money issues were not the real problem; they were only the symptom. Winning the lottery put a Band-Aid on the problem, but it did not cure it. And once the Band-Aid wore out (the lottery money was spent), they found themselves again in a familiar state of bondage. It turns out they themselves were the root problem.

There is nothing wrong with wanting to be saved, but wanting to be saved does not equal wanting to be changed. So when I read the Scriptures as though salvation is the central theme, will I find the cure to the root problem—me!?

As we explore what the Gospel is, I want to start by getting your thoughts on the question. So this next part involves a little participation on your part. Get a piece of paper or use the lines below and jot down the basic parts of the Gospel. I just want the main points. Pretend you only have a few minutes with a person who has never heard the Gospel. What would you tell them? Remember, just the main points!

_____

_____

I've had people from all over the world perform this exercise. I usually receive the same general responses wherever I go. They include one or more of the following:

1. God loves you and wants to forgive your sins.

2. You have sinned, so you need God's mercy to forgive you.

3. Jesus died on the cross to save you from your sins.

4. He rose!

Oftentimes, we even forget about point 4—He rose!—ending our presentation with His death. Let's not do that, because without His resurrection, "our preaching is empty and your faith is also empty." 1 Corinthians 15:14. Let it never be!

But let's say we include each of these four points. While they are great answers, notice that all focus on the work of the cross. That is true in nearly 100% of the responses I hear to the question, "What is the Gospel?"

I agree that these four points capture important aspects of the gospel, but is there more to the Good News? Let me approach this question from a different angle. Say that you are an unbeliever and I'm proclaiming the Gospel to you. I tell you that God loves *you*, Jesus came to earth for *you*, died to save *you*, and rose again to secure a place in heaven for *you*. As the listener, who would you say is the subject of our conversation? You!

If that makes you squirm a bit, we're on the right track. So let me ask it again, is there more to the conversation than me and you? Yes, I believe so. Let's dig in.

B.   The Gospel

As we begin exploring how the Bible defines the Gospel, turn in your Bible to Luke 18. No, really, please open your Bible so you can see with your own eyes that what I tell you is true.

Before we get into the scripture, let's talk about when and to whom Jesus is speaking in Luke 18. First, the when: In this chapter, Jesus is at the end of His earthly ministry. The majority of theologians agree that this chapter describes events occurring only four days before Jesus' crucifixion. Most of them believe these events took place the very day He entered Jerusalem as the Lamb of God destined for sacrifice.

Second, the who: Jesus' audience is the twelve disciples. They have followed Him throughout His earthly ministry. They ate with Him, slept next to Him, and heard His sermons. He took them aside and explained His parables, saying, "To you has been given the secret of the Kingdom of God, but for those outside everything is in parables." Mark 4:11. For over three years, these were the men closest to Jesus and His mission. They know His facial expressions, His tastes . . . everything.

With this in mind that the context of this chapter was Jesus talking to His disciples, four days before His death, let's read Luke 18:31-33: "Then He took the twelve aside and said to them, 'Behold, we are going up to Jerusalem, and all things that are written by the prophets concerning the Son of Man will be accomplished. For He will be delivered to the Gentiles and will be mocked and insulted and spit upon. They will scourge Him and kill Him. And the third day He will rise again.'"

So Jesus tells His disciples about His upcoming work on the cross. He proclaims He is going to die and rise again. This is the Gospel that is proclaimed today in a nutshell.

Let's now examine how the disciples respond to Jesus' declaration of His impending death and resurrection. Luke tells us their reaction in the very next verse, Luke 18:34: "But they *understood none of these things*; this saying was *hidden* from them, and they *did not know* the things which were spoken."

What is it that was hidden from them? The disciples of Jesus Christ, who had been following Him for three years, understood none of the things Jesus told them about His impending death and resurrection—what we today call the Gospel.

Here's how much they didn't understand the cross at this point: Peter actually rebukes Jesus for saying that He would be crucified. Matthew 16:22. Was Peter living a partial conversation at this point—hearing only the facts that appealed to him? That is, while he understood that Jesus is the Messiah, the King of Israel, did he have ears for the facts that didn't sound good (like Jesus' impending death)? What did this lead him to do? For one, it prompted him to cut off the ear of one of the soldiers who came to arrest Jesus, despite Jesus telling the disciples this was coming. John 18:10. Peter wanted to usher in the kingdom of God his way, not Jesus' way.

I'm not throwing stones at Peter for failing to understand Jesus' words of His coming death and resurrection—Luke says it was hidden from him. In fact, Luke says it three times using different words:

1. "They understood none of these things";

2. "This saying was hidden from them"; and

3. "They did not know the things which were spoken."

Why does the Holy Spirit prompt Luke to write that the disciples were taught on three occasions about Jesus going to the cross, only to have them remain clueless? Why did He want us, the reader today, to understand that this work, the Gospel as we know it, was hidden from them?

Let's jump back to Luke 9, which takes place about a year and a half before Luke 18. Here, Luke says that Jesus "called His twelve disciples together and gave them power and authority over all the demons, and to cure diseases." Luke 9:1. So, Jesus sent them out, and "they began going throughout the villages, *preaching the gospel* and healing everywhere." Luke 9:6.

This scripture says the disciples preached the gospel! But hang on, we know that in Luke 18, which takes place after Luke 9, the disciples could not comprehend the work of the cross—what we today preach as the whole of the Gospel. What does this mean? If the disciples did not know that Jesus was going to die and rise again, then what "Gospel" did the disciples preach when they went out two by two?

Before we go any further, let me affirm that Jesus' work on the cross is key to the Gospel. If a man was preaching a cross-less Gospel from our pulpits today, we would proclaim him a heretic and kick him out. I'm not telling you differently. We cannot preach the Gospel without the work of the cross.

But I believe there is more to the Gospel than what we commonly proclaim. Limiting the explanation of the Gospel to the cross alone can actually lead us to misunderstand the Gospel because we heard only a part of the whole truth. The cross is a key, but the One that went to the cross is the Key! Having a partial conversation about the cross can wind up a vain conversation if we don't find the right perspective. We can act as though His work on the cross is centered around us instead of God.

In seeking to escape partial conversation, we do not take away from our current understanding of the Gospel; instead, we come to a fuller understanding.

1. Who did Jesus say He is?

We saw in the book of Luke that the disciples did preach the Gospel before Jesus' death and resurrection. And when they preached, people were healed everywhere. Yet they did not understand that Jesus would die and rise again for the sin of the world. So what was the Gospel the disciples preached? With no understanding of Jesus' impending death and resurrection, what was the Good News they proclaimed?

To reach the answer, I believe we must answer another question first. I know, this chapter has lots of questions! But this is the greatest question of all time. Even today, this question is asked in churches, mosques, homes, schools, universities, offices, bars, locker rooms, and around the world: "Who is Jesus?"

Some say He is a good teacher, humanitarian, prophet, a fake, never existed, cultist, friend, an angel, etc. "But who do you say that I am?" He asks.

In John 18, the apostle John tells us about the Jewish leaders bringing Jesus to Pontius Pilate, the Roman governor of Judea (the region where Jerusalem is located). It's important to understand that Pilate is not a Jew. Most Bible commentaries say that Pilate was made governor over the Jews in Jerusalem as punishment for something he did wrong in his previous position.

Pilate probably didn't like Jews, and dealt with them only when necessary to enforce the law. This is why the Jewish leaders brought Jesus to Pilate. They wanted Jesus executed, but they needed Pilate to give his stamp of approval for this capital punishment.

Since Pilate didn't interact much with Jews, he probably didn't know much about Jesus except what the Jewish leaders told him: "We found this fellow perverting the nation, and forbidding to pay taxes to Caesar, saying that He himself is Christ, a King." Luke 23:2. If Pilate's response to this intrusion into his day seems confused, it's likely because he was confused. The Jewish leaders probably didn't often ask Pilate to kill one of their own.

Since the Jewish leaders wanted to kill Jesus because of who He claimed to be, Pilate wants to know the same thing we do: Who is Jesus? Specifically, Pilate asked "Are You a king then?" John 18:37. This is a very interesting question. Even more interesting, we get to hear Jesus' response to the question we're trying to answer. This is a good cue for you and me to pay attention.

Jesus answered Pilate, "You say rightly that I am a king. For this cause I was born, and for this cause I came into the world, that I should bear witness to the truth. Everyone who is of the truth hears My voice." John 18:37. Pilate asked one question, but Jesus answers two questions: who He is and why He came into the world. We will look at both.

But first, who does Jesus say hears His voice? Those who are of the truth! Many would respond by asking the same follow-up question that Pilate asked in the next verse: "What is truth?" For many today, and maybe for Pilate then, truth is relative.

In reality, Jesus is the Truth. But Truth involves many facts, so where do you start when seeking it? For example, Jesus is the son of man, can walk on water, is the healer, but none of these facts alone captures the whole truth. Let's look again at Pilate's interrogation. He thought he was deciding whether Jesus would live or die. And the question he asked was not if Jesus is a savior, friend, or father (although He is all of those things). What did he ask?

The foundational question Pilate asked is if Jesus is a king. Jesus replies by saying, "You say rightly that I am a king." John 18:37. What is a king? Let's look at how three dictionaries define "king":

Random House Kernerman Webster's College Dictionary[2]:

> 1. a male sovereign or monarch; a man who holds by life tenure, and usu. by hereditary right, the chief authority over a country and people.
>
> 2. a person or thing preeminent in its class: the king of actors.

Collins English Dictionary[3]:

> 1. (Government, Politics & Diplomacy) a male sovereign prince who is the official ruler of an independent state; monarch.
>
> 2. a ruler or chief: king of the fairies.
>
> 3. a person, animal, or thing considered as the best or most important of its kind

The American Heritage Dictionary[4]:

> 1. A male sovereign.

---

[2] Random House Kernerman Webster's College Dictionary (Tel Aviv: K Dictionaries, 2010).
[3] Collins English Dictionary – Complete and Unabridged (New York: HarperCollins, 2003).
[4] The American Heritage Dictionary of the English Language, Fourth Edition (Boston: Houghton Mifflin Harcourt, 2009).

2. One that is supreme or preeminent in a particular group, category, or sphere.

3. King

a. The perfect, omniscient, omnipotent being; God.

b. Christianity Jesus.

I love all three of these dictionary definitions. Each one helps us get a better understanding of this word, "king." Within its full definition is so much heavenly revelation.

A king is the official ruler, preeminent in his class, considered as the best or most important of his kind, and supreme over all. A king is different than, for example, the President of the United States. The presidency is an office. The president receives the office through the people, and he is in office for the people. When his term is over, he is no longer president. In contrast, a king is not an office. He is king by birth; that is, by hereditary right. The king becomes king through inheritance, by royal blood. In other words, he is king because of who he is—the son of the king. He is king for life, and with respect to Jesus, He is King for Eternity. So, a king is not just an office. A king is not just what he does; it is who he is.

Wow! This is our Jesus! The Christ who lives today and forevermore, Amen! The Truth will set us free. What truth will set us free? That Jesus is the King.

2. Who do you say Jesus is?

Jesus knew the question, "Who is Jesus?" was being asked in His time on earth, and He knew it would continue to be asked today. So He asked His disciples, "Who do men say that I, the Son of Man, am?" Matthew 16:13. The disciples answered, "Some say John the Baptist, some Elijah, and others Jeremiah or one of the prophets." Matthew 16:14. Note that each suggestion referred to men of the past. Men who had a deep relationship with Father God. But none declared Jesus as His own.

The people were trying to describe Jesus through their paradigm instead of God's paradigm. Many of us today do the same. We try to use our logic to reason out who we think Jesus is, rather than getting God's perspective of Him. We use facts instead of the Truth to come to our conclusions about who He is.

The first time Jesus asked the disciples about who He is, He does not begin by inquiring of them personally. He asks about what others were saying about Him. But after He asks about other peoples' opinion, He turns the question back to the disciples and asks them directly, "But who do you say that I am?" Matthew 16:15.

This is the question Pilate had to answer. This was also his opportunity. He asked the right question, "Are You the King of the Jews?" John 18:33. Jesus responded, "Are you speaking for yourself about this, or did others tell you this concerning Me." John 18:34. In other words, "Pilate, would you like Me to be your King? Now's your chance!"

While Pilate may have begun with little knowledge of Jesus, he gained more before rendering judgment. Pilate's wife sent word to him, saying, "Have nothing to do with that just Man, for I have suffered many things today in a dream because of Him." Matthew 27:19. Then, Pilate heard the Jews say that Jesus "made himself the Son of God." John 19:7. This news made Pilate "even more afraid." John 19:8 (ESV).

But even though Pilate was afraid of Jesus, he had a competing fear: Caesar, the king of the Roman Empire. The Jewish authorities played into Pilate's fear of Caesar when

Pilate tried to release Jesus. They cried out to Pilate, "If you release this man, you are not a friend of Caesar's." John 19:12. So Pilate had a choice—would he bow to the king of an earthly kingdom or the King of a heavenly kingdom?

Pilate thought he was deciding whether Jesus would live or die. But, really, Pilate was deciding whether Pilate would live or die—that is, whether he would have everlasting life with Jesus or suffer everlasting death apart from Jesus. He had to decide whether to accept Jesus as King or whether he would say, like the chief priests of the Jews, "we have no king but Caesar." John 19:15.

Pilate tried to absolve himself of responsibility by washing his hands of Jesus and turning Him over to the Jews to do with as they pleased. But Jesus said that we don't have the luxury of that indecision. He said, "Whoever is not with me is against me, and whoever does not gather with me scatters." Matthew 12:30.

Church, do you realize that when you stand before God Most High it will not matter what your pastors, parents, friends, teachers, or anyone else said about who He is. It will be you and God, and you will not be able to say, "My Pastor said . . . ." We have this life and this life alone to confess the right answer to Jesus' question, "Who do you say that I am?"

3.   Salvation by revelation

In seeking to understand who Jesus is, let us ask the Father's perspective. I want God's view, not man's. I want a heavenly perspective, not an earthly perspective. We need to pray for the Spirit of wisdom and revelation so that we might know Him, rather than just knowing of Him. Ephesians 1:16-17.

When Jesus asked the disciples who they thought He was, they understood He was no longer asking them to regurgitate the opinions of others. Now they had to answer for themselves. Peter steps up, saying, "You are the Christ, the Son of the living God." Matthew 16:16.

Peter's answer may not seem like a big deal to us. That's probably because we say Jesus Christ so much without realizing the indescribable importance of what we are saying. Many say it as if it is His last name—Mr. Christ, but that is not what it means.

Christ means "anointed one," which is a reference to the one prophesied in the Old Testament who would be both king and priest. The anointed one of whom David wrote, "You are a priest forever according to the order of Melchizedek." Psalm 110:4. Melchizedek was not just a priest; the Bible also describes Melchizedek as the king of righteousness and peace. Hebrews 7:2.

Like Melchizedek, Jesus, the anointed one, is the great high priest (Hebrews 4:14) and the one who would sit on the throne as King forever and ever (Hebrews 1:8). So when we say "Christ," we are really saying that Jesus is the priestly King who will receive the nations as His inheritance and the ends of the earth for His possession. Psalm 2:8.

Many Jewish people understood the Messiah's kingly role much more than His priestly role. They believed the Messiah would deliver them from Roman rule. He was not a guy who would first die in sacrifice for their sins, then only later, at some unspecified point in the future, establish His kingdom. With this mindset, it's not surprising that even after Jesus' death and resurrection, the apostles so frequently crown the name Jesus not just with the description "Christ," but also "Lord." Here are just a few examples from Paul's letters:

> Grace to you, and peace, from God our Father, and from the *Lord Jesus Christ*. Blessed be the God and

38

Father of our Lord Jesus Christ, who has blessed us with every spiritual blessing in the heavenly places in Christ. Ephesians 1:2-3.

Grace be to you and peace from God the Father, and from our *Lord Jesus Christ*. Galatians 1:3.

Blessed be God, even the Father of our *Lord Jesus Christ*, the Father of mercies, and the God of all comfort. 2 Corinthians 1:3.

Let's look at the definition of "lord": "one having power and authority over others: a ruler by hereditary right or preeminence to whom service and obedience are due."[5] Do you see the similarity to the definitions of "king" we looked at earlier? By describing Jesus as "Lord," Paul was recognizing that Jesus Christ, the Anointed One, is the rightful ruler, the King.

So when Peter said that Jesus was the Christ, the Son of the living God, he was making a big statement. And we see just how big it was when Jesus responds, "Blessed are you, Simon Bar-Jonah, for flesh and blood has not revealed this to you, but my Father who is in heaven." Matthew 16:17. Jesus put the disciples on the spot, and the Father saved Peter by giving him the answer.

Just like Peter, we must all receive salvation by revelation. We must do more than confess Jesus as a great teacher or even as an anointed miracle worker. To be saved, we must confess Jesus as Lord. That is, the one having all power and authority by virtue of His position as the only begotten Son of God. We must confess Jesus as the God who created the heavens and the earth.

---

[5] "Lord," Merriam-Webster, accessed Nov. 16, 2016, http://www.merriam-webster.com/dictionary/lord.

We Christians often cite Paul's statement in Romans that, "If you confess with your mouth that Jesus is Lord and believe in your heart that God raised him from the dead, you will be saved." Romans 10:9 (ESV). But what does it mean to confess Jesus as *Lord*? Paul goes on to say that "everyone who calls on the name of the Lord will be saved." Romans 10:13. He's quoting Joel 2:32, which states, "And it shall come to pass that everyone who calls on the name of the LORD shall be saved." Notice that's "LORD" in all capitals, meaning Yahweh, the one true God. So Paul identifies Jesus with Yahweh. This is why the book of Revelation can identify Jesus as the King of kings and Lord of lords. Any response to the question, "Who is Jesus?" that falls short of confessing Jesus as Yahweh (that is, God in the flesh) falls short of the Biblical confession of salvation.

Confessing Jesus as Yahweh is easier said than done. It cannot be done through man's decision alone. It cannot be done through mere knowledge of facts. In fact, there is only one way we are able to confess that Jesus is the Christ. It is only through revelation. And that revelation comes not from flesh and blood, but from Father God. Matthew 16:17. No one can come to Jesus unless the Father draws him. John 6:44.

4.   **Why did Jesus come?**

You may have by now forgotten that we began our quest trying to figure out what Gospel the disciples preached before understanding the cross. In that quest, we answered a different question, the greatest question of all time—who is Jesus?—and the answer is "the Christ, the Son of the living God!" We found the Truth is that He is King.

I promise we will answer our first question, but to continue in our quest we need to ask, yes, another question. Why did Jesus Christ come to earth? What was the reason He was born here on this sinful planet? Why did the Most High God come to earth as man, born of woman?

There are many reasons, and therefore there can be many right answers. Paul, when talking to a believer, his spiritual son Timothy, writes: "This is a faithful saying, and worthy of all acceptance, that Christ Jesus came into the world to save sinners, of whom I am chief." 1 Timothy 1:15.

This is so true. Jesus Christ did come to save sinners. As Paul wrote in Romans, we have all sinned. This was actually a shock to Jews, who believed they were pure until they committed an act of sin. As for me, I was full of sin, yet He came to save me before I was even born!

So Jesus did come to save sinners, but is that the big-picture reason? How do we figure out the big-picture reason among all the subsidiary reasons? Maybe an example will help us along. In 2008, the real-estate market in the United States collapsed after several years of rapidly increasing prices, causing home values to plummet in many regions of the country. Different economists offer different reasons for the rise and subsequent collapse in prices, including greedy banks lending customers more money than they could realistically pay back; lustful customers buying more expensive houses than they could afford; and government policies dictated by special-interest groups rather than good judgment. All of these are probably true, but each of them misses the larger reason: America needs Jesus. If our nation feared God, the banks would be much less likely to prey on uneducated customers, customers wouldn't be driven by the idolatry of covetousness, and our government would govern by God's wisdom rather than man's. I can't wait for the fullness of His Kingdom with His return!

For so long I was like these economists. I had all these reasons why Jesus came and why He died on the cross. But I didn't understand the big-picture reason. If we want to discover Jesus' main reason for coming, we should look first to His words. We must inquire first of the subject of the conversation before looking to those talking about the subject.

Let's look again to Jesus' response to Pilate's question in John 18, "Are you a King?" Remember that Jesus actually answered two questions: (1) "You say rightly that I am a king"; and (2) "For this cause I was born, and for this cause I came into the world, that I should bear witness to the truth." John 18:37. The answer to the question, "Who is Jesus?" also answers why He came. He came into the world not only to be King, but also to bear witness to this truth that He is the King.

This is a game changer. It changes the context of His coming. If His main purpose in coming was to reveal Himself as the King, then the subject of the conversation is not our salvation. Instead, the conversation is about His kingship.

Our salvation is a consequence of His kingship. Because He is King, He had authority to lay down His life in sacrifice for us, and authority to take it up again. John 10:18. It is by this authority, which He received from Father God, that we are pulled from our sin and ushered into His kingdom. Paul explains this, saying that God "has delivered us from the power of darkness and conveyed us into the kingdom of the Son of His love, in whom we have redemption through His blood, the forgiveness of sins." Colossians 1:13-14.

Let's look at another scripture where Jesus says why He came. Near the beginning of His ministry, Jesus came home to Nazareth, the town where He was raised. Jesus went into the synagogue, opened the book of Isaiah and read, "The Spirit of the Lord is upon Me, because He has anointed me to preach the gospel to the poor." Luke 4:18 (quoting Isaiah

61:1). Jesus then told the assembly, "Today this Scripture is fulfilled in your hearing." Luke 4:21. So, here, Jesus expressly states that His mission included preaching the gospel.

With that in mind, look at Jesus' words a few verses later in Luke 4: "I must preach the kingdom of God to the other cities also, for I was sent for this purpose." Luke 4:43 (NASB). We saw in John 18 that Jesus was sent to serve as a witness to the Truth that He is King. In Luke 4, we see that another aspect of His mission was proclaiming His kingdom—not just in one place, but to the other cities also.

Remember that we were trying to figure out how the disciples could preach the gospel in Luke 9 when they still didn't understand Jesus' impending death and resurrection as late as Luke 18. Let's go back to that passage in Luke 9 and look at one additional verse that sheds light on what Jesus told the disciples to preach: "Then He called His twelve disciples together . . . and sent them to *preach the kingdom of God*." Luke 9:1-2. So, four verses later, when Luke says the disciples "departed and went through the towns, preaching the gospel" (Luke 9:6), he's saying the disciples preached the kingdom of God.

Let's take a look at what that gospel of the kingdom of God entails.

5.   The kingdom: the King and His culture

We need to understand this "kingdom" Jesus came to proclaim. The word "kingdom" is intense and full of deep revelations. A king will rule over his country. But the King of kings holds in His hand the very universe. The heavens are the work of His fingers, and He set the stars in their place. Psalm 8:3. "All things were made through Him, and without Him nothing was made that was made." John 1:3. Jesus rules over the entire universe. The heavens are His throne and the

43

earth His footstool! Isaiah 66:1.

To get a picture of what that means, let's break "kingdom" down into its two parts: "king" and "dom." We already talked about what it means to be king. Now, let's look at the meaning of the suffix "dom": "a suffix forming nouns that refer to domain (kingdom)." So, a "kingdom" refers to the domain of the king.

"Domain," in turn, refers to the territory controlled by a single government or king. But "domain" refers to more than just physical territory. The king's reign extends not just over the physical borders of his land, but also the culture that exists within his land. So when we talk about the king's domain, this includes not just his authority over the external borders of the kingdom, but also his authority over the culture of the kingdom—the *what*, *why*, and *how* of His dominion.

Jesus came into the world to bear witness to the truth that He is King and to proclaim His kingdom. In other words, He came to proclaim who He is and the culture of His reign.

If we're going to enter Jesus' kingdom, we must accept His culture. Let's look at how Jesus says to do that. In Jesus' first message to the crowds after returning from forty days of fasting in the wilderness, He says something very simple: "Repent, for the kingdom of heaven is at hand." Matthew 4:17. He did not say, "Repent because I am going to die on the cross." Instead, Jesus began His preaching by calling for repentance because the King and His culture had arrived. In other words, He called on the Jews (who thought they were of God by their physical descent from Abraham) to turn away from *their* culture because *His* culture was at hand. He wanted them to hear this message of repentance.

Mark's gospel account gives a similar description, but he

adds another element—belief. "Now after John was put in prison, Jesus came into Galilee, preaching the gospel of the kingdom of God, and saying, 'The time is fulfilled, and the kingdom of God is at hand. Repent, and believe in the gospel.'" Mark 1:14-15. Again, Jesus did not yet mention the cross, but announced that the time is fulfilled; the kingdom of God is at hand. And He called on them to repent and believe "the gospel of the kingdom of God."

This is the same gospel the disciples went out preaching in Luke 9, before they understood the cross. This might prompt you to ask whether they (and Jesus) were preaching a different gospel than the post-cross gospel. That's a good question to consider, so let's look at it now.

6.   There's only one gospel

There is only one gospel. Jesus says in Mark 1:15 to believe "the gospel." This is a powerful statement. Sometimes, little words are critical. In Mark 1:15, the use of "the" before "gospel" is one of those occasions. In grammar, we call "the" a definite article, while an indefinite article would be "a." We use a definite article in front of a noun when we believe that our audience knows exactly what the noun refers to, because there is only one of it.

For example, in America, we say, "*the* President is visiting Georgia," because our audience knows there is only one President of the United States. But if we were talking about a university president, we might say, "a president is visiting Georgia," because there are many university presidents and we aren't identifying which one we're specifically talking about. So, in this example, the difference between a definite article and an indefinite article is the difference between talking about the one and only president versus one of many presidents.

Like the "president" example, when Jesus proclaims that we are to believe "*the* gospel," He is announcing the one and only gospel. Lest you think I'm placing too much weight on the difference between Jesus calling on people to believe *the* gospel instead of *a* gospel, let's look at how the Bible characterizes the gospel proclaimed by the apostles and early church. While the New Testament authors often simply refer to "the gospel," we'll see that they confirm they're talking about Jesus' gospel of the kingdom.

Let's start by looking at Jesus' instructions to the disciples after His resurrection. He told them, "Go therefore and make disciples of all the nations, baptizing them in the name of the Father and of the Son and of the Holy Spirit, teaching them to observe all things that I have commanded you." Matthew 28:19-20. Mark's gospel puts it like this: "Go into all the world and preach the gospel to every creature." Mark 16:15. Was this gospel Jesus wanted the disciples to proclaim the same "gospel of the kingdom" that Jesus preached during His ministry? Let's go back a bit in Matthew and see if we can get a clue.

In Matthew 24, which records events that took place during the week Jesus was crucified, the disciples ask Jesus, "What will be the sign of Your coming, and of the end of the age?" Matthew 24:3. In addition to describing signs of the end of the age, Jesus describes an event that will take place before the end of the age: "And this *gospel of the kingdom* will be preached in all the world as a witness to all the nations, and then the end will come." Matthew 24:14. Do you think Jesus' reference to "this gospel of the kingdom" being preached as a witness to all the nations that it is indeed the gospel He wanted His disciples to proclaim in fulfillment of the great commission?

Let's see what other instructions Jesus gave the disciples after the resurrection. In the first verses of Acts, Luke tells us that the risen Jesus "presented Himself alive after His suffering by many infallible proofs, being seen by them during forty days and speaking to them of the things pertaining to the *kingdom of God.*" Acts 1:3. So Jesus didn't just proclaim the kingdom *before* His death on the cross; He kept proclaiming it *after* His resurrection.

What did the disciples do after Jesus ascended to heaven? They followed His instruction to preach the kingdom. In Acts 8, we read how persecution spread the gospel after most disciples fled Jerusalem in response to oppression: "those who were scattered went everywhere preaching the word." Acts 8:4 One of those was Philip, who "went down to the city of Samaria and preached Christ to them." Acts 8:5. A few verses later, Luke expands on Philip's preaching, telling us about people who "believed Philip as he preached the things concerning the kingdom of God and the name of Jesus Christ." Acts 8:12. What happened next? "Both men and women were baptized." Acts 8:12. Luke equates their belief in the kingdom of God and the name of Jesus Christ with the saving faith that precedes baptism.

Philip wasn't alone in preaching the gospel of the kingdom. That's what Paul preached, too. In Acts 19, we read about Paul's journey to Ephesus, where he "spoke boldly for three months" in the synagogue, "reasoning and persuading concerning the things of the kingdom of God." Acts 19:8. Luke again equates proclaiming the kingdom of God with the gospel, as he goes on to say that "some were hardened and did not believe, but spoke evil of the Way before the multitude." Acts 19:9. In other words, these Ephesians' failure to believe Paul's bold speech about the kingdom of God meant they rejected the Gospel.

Luke tells us more about Paul preaching the Gospel of the Kingdom. In Acts 20, Luke describes an emotional meeting between Paul and the Ephesian elders; emotional because

Paul told them it was the last time they would see him. Paul says that the ministry he received "from the Lord Jesus [was] to testify to the gospel of the grace of God." Acts 20:24. How did Paul characterize this gospel of grace that Jesus commissioned him to proclaim? He called it "preaching the kingdom of God." Acts 20:25. And in the next verse, Paul says that because he preached the kingdom of God, "I testify to you this day that I am innocent of the blood of all men." Acts 20:26.

Think about that for a minute. Paul says he fulfilled the ministry he received directly from the Lord Jesus by preaching the Kingdom of God. What was Paul's ministry? In Ephesians, he says, "Of this gospel I was made a minister according to the gift of God's grace." Ephesians 3:7.

Paul didn't discriminate. He preached the same gospel of the kingdom to both Jews and Gentiles. When Paul testified before King Agrippa in Acts 26, he said, "Therefore, King Agrippa, I was not disobedient to the heavenly vision, but declared *first to those in Damascus and in Jerusalem*, and throughout all the region of Judea, and *then to the Gentiles*, that they should repent, turn to God, and do works befitting repentance." Acts 26:19-20.

Luke then specifically ties Paul's message to Jesus' gospel of the kingdom in the concluding chapter of Acts, which refers to Paul's arrival in Rome as a prisoner. Luke says that after Paul reached out to the Roman Jews, "many came to him at his lodging, to whom he explained and solemnly testified of the *kingdom of God*, persuading them concerning Jesus from both the Law of Moses and the Prophets, from morning till evening." Acts 28:23.

But Paul didn't preach the kingdom of God only to the Jews. After some Jews believed and some didn't, Paul said, "Therefore let it be known to you that the salvation of God has been sent to the Gentiles, and they will hear it!" Acts 28:28. Luke tells us that Paul dwelt at least two years in a rented house in Rome, where he "received all who came to him, *preaching the kingdom of God* and teaching the things which concern the Lord Jesus Christ with all confidence." Acts 28:30-31.

Jesus came to proclaim *the* one Gospel, the Gospel of the Kingdom, and that is the same Gospel Paul and the other apostles preached in accordance with Jesus' instructions. Mark 16:15. Without this realization that there is only one Gospel—the Gospel of the Kingdom, we won't fully understand what Jesus Himself calls us to believe.

7.   Believing the Gospel of the Kingdom

What does Jesus mean when He says that we need to believe the Gospel? We saw in Mark 1:14 that Jesus came preaching the Gospel of the Kingdom of God. So, according to Mark, the Gospel *is* the Kingdom of God. Jesus then says, "The time is fulfilled, and *the kingdom of God* is at hand." The Gospel is King Jesus and His culture, and it is here to be grasped by those who believe. If you believe it, you will grasp it.

Let's zoom in on what it means to believe. The Greek word translated "believe" here can more specifically be understood as entrusting yourself to that which you are believing. Jesus called on us to entrust ourselves to the Gospel of the Kingdom. Think about what that means. If you place your trust in something, it affects your behavior. If you entrust yourself to the Kingdom, the King and His culture, your behavior will reflect His culture. "Trust in the LORD with all your heart, and do not depend on your own understanding. In all your ways acknowledge him, and he will make your paths straight." Proverbs 3:5-6 (ISV).

Now is the time to accept the King's culture, because the King is coming back. And when He does, what we do not yet see will become apparent: the Father has put all things in subjection under His feet. Hebrews 2:8. Who will take His arrival as good news? Those who believe He will return—they will be wise and faithful servants, acting out their faith by learning to do His culture, and therefore becoming a living expression of His culture, even while He remains out of sight. Matthew 24:45.

When the signs of the King's return appear, those who trusted in Him will lift their heads because their redemption draws near. Luke 21:25-28. How about the wicked servant who used the King's absence as an excuse to ignore His culture and instead conform to the world's culture by pursuing his personal desires? Matthew 24:48-49. He will be ashamed at the King's coming, seeking shelter in the very rocks of the earth. Luke 21:26; Revelation 6:15-17. But, ultimately, even that shelter will flee from him. Revelation 20:11. And then there is no respite from the wrath of God for those who rejected the King. Luke 19:27. So let's not delay. Let's put our minds on Him, demonstrating that our trust is in Him. Trusting in Him gives a peace from Heaven, along with an incredible desire for His return. Isaiah 26:3.

8.   Seeking the revelation of the King

We often hear that people are "seeking," but what are they seeking? It's so easy to get bogged down seeking after physical needs (or, more often, physical wants). I want to make it clear that God loves to meet our needs. But our relationship cannot be motivated by those needs; it must be motivated by His presence. But let's say we're trying to move past our physical needs and seek a relationship with God. Where do we begin? Are we to seek first our salvation? Are we to seek first the blessings and rewards? Do we seek first His friendship, or His fatherhood?

Jesus gave us the answer: "*seek first* His kingdom and His righteousness, and all these things will be added to you." Matthew 6:33. This is critical—Jesus says to seek His Kingdom first! While Paul says that the work of Christ on the cross is of first importance, our pursuit must begin by chasing Him as our King, His culture as our culture. Yes, the cross is essential—it allows entrance to the destination. But it is not the destination itself. He is our destination! Our search for eternity with God must begin by seeking the Kingdom of God—now. Actually, eternal life is knowing God. John 17:3. Only when we seek God's Kingdom can we grasp the fullness of Jesus' work on the cross. Because when we walk in revelation of the One who did the work, it brings more power to the work that He has done. Without revelation of who He is, we will miss the fullness of the cross.

There is a very popular verse that many believers can quote: "Where there is no vision, the people perish." Proverbs 29:18 (KJV). The Hebrew word translated as "vision" is *chazon*. Strong's Concordance defines this more fully as "a sight (mentally), that is, a dream, revelation, or oracle: vision." The New King James Version translates the verse this way: "Where there is no revelation . . ." So without revelation, the people will perish. That is powerful! The New King James Version helps us understand that this "vision" we must have involves receiving a revelation.

People who have a vision that isn't formed from a continuous revelation of who Christ is will perish even if they cast out demons, heal the sick, or prophesy. Mathew 7:21-23. We must seek the King and His culture continually as our first priority, resulting in indescribable revelations of Him. As our understanding and knowledge of who He is increases at Heavenly levels, we will begin to comprehend the fullness of what He has done, is doing and, will do.

We can gain insight into seeking first God's Kingdom by

looking to earthly examples. In many foreign countries, the people revere their ruler. Even the people of North Korea honor their dictator absolutely, even if it is done out of absolute fear. Another example is Thailand. When one of my former students spent a couple months there, she was struck by the love the Thai people have for their king. She had never seen anything like it. She said the Thai people even hold their hand in a certain posture when pointing to a picture of him; otherwise, it is considered disrespectful. The king even gets special words to describe his body parts—the words for the king's hands and feet are different than the words used to refer to everyone else's hands and feet.

The Thais have experienced an authoritarian king, so they understand what Jesus meant when He said that the kings of the nations lord it over them. When my student explained that Jesus wasn't merely a man who gave his life for the people, but the *King* who gave His life for His people, they were blown away by the weight of those words. Who could imagine such a thing!

I pray for a paradigm like the Thais. I want my King to be so set apart in my heart and mind that I need a whole separate vocabulary for everything about Him. The reverence the Thais have for their earthly king gave them special insight to the magnitude of Jesus' sacrificial work on the cross. That's what the revelation of Jesus as King does for our understanding of the cross.

The person who will follow God is the one who understands this truth that He is King. Jesus said that those of the truth will know His voice. In the Gospel of John, we read, "the sheep follow [the shepherd], for they know his voice." John 10:4 [ESV]. Jesus said, "I am the good shepherd." John 10:11 [ESV]. Who knows the good Shepherd's voice? Those who have revelation of the Truth that Jesus is King! What will be their response to this revelation of the Truth? Repenting, with the result of receiving His Kingdom.

This is why He came into the world—to pronounce and demonstrate that He is the King, and to give an invitation to receive His Kingdom (Heavenly culture)! This understanding brings a paradigm shift. When we receive the revelation that He is the King and came to bear witness of that truth, we will hear His voice and become empowered through grace to live His Kingdom life here on earth as it is in Heaven.

This is the same revelation that Peter received that allowed him to say, "You are the Christ, the Son of the living God." Matthew 16:16. Jesus tells Peter that no man revealed this to him. Rather, Jesus said it was revealed by "My Father who is in Heaven." Matthew 16:17. This revelation that Jesus is the Christ, or, in other words, the King, is essential to receiving salvation.

After explaining that Peter's revelation came from the Father, Jesus then says He plans to build His church (the believers themselves, not a building or denomination) on the rock of this revelation of who He *is*. Jesus does not say that it will be built on what He does. We must avoid just falling in love with just Jesus' past acts and future power (what He does), but never really falling in love with Him. This can happen when we never receive a true revelation of Him—of who He is, and instead just want more miracles.

We don't necessarily have a revelation of who He is simply because He reveals His power to us. Remember that the miracles and the supernatural acts of God are called *signs* and *wonders*. The signs and wonders are an invitation to seek the One that is completing them —they are signs pointing to Him; they cause people to wonder about Him. But believing He performed the signs wasn't the same as believing in Him. So many people followed Jesus during His earthly ministry to see His power, but denied Him and ran away when He presented Himself "weak" to Rome. They loved seeing His power, but they did not receive the revelation of Him necessary to keep them in Him.

Jesus also tells Peter that the gates of hell (or, in Greek, "Hades") will not prevail against the church when it is built on the revelation of who Jesus is. Matthew 16:17. This is a big deal. Jesus told Capernaum, a city that did not repent even after seeing His mighty works, that it would "be brought down to Hades." Matthew 11:23 (ESV).

But Jesus says, "I have the keys of Death and Hades." Revelation 1:18 (ESV). And praise God that He uses those keys! The gates of Hades will not hold those who have a revelation of the Christ and put their trust in Him. Paul said that to die is to "be with Christ." Philippians 1:23.

Not only that, Jesus, in encouraging us to be zealous for Him, said, "To him who overcomes I will grant to sit with Me on My throne, as I also overcame and sat down with My Father on His throne." Revelation 3:21. Jesus gave this word specifically to the early church in a city called Laodicea, but He followed it by saying, "He who has an ear, let him hear what the Spirit says to the churches." Revelation 3:22. When reading such a passage, we know that Jesus was not looking to see if people had physical ears, but if they were hungry for deeper truth called revelation. Do we have an ear? If so, let's talk about how we can overcome: through the revelation of Jesus as the Christ. Through this revelation, we receive the grace (that is, divine empowerment) to overcome—to be victorious. The revelation of Him provides protection and strength against the enemy and his domain of death. AMEN!

The time has come to quit trying to build the church on the shifting sand of human wisdom, and instead allow Jesus to build His church on the rock of revelation—He is the

Christ! This will create a powerful and strong warrior bride! Not an insecure bride who is trying to hide in a cave of comfort, but one mighty in confidence because she knows the One who loves her and protects her and empowers her—the Christ; the King of Kings; the Alpha and Omega; the Beginning and the End; He who was, who is, and who is to come! Amen!

Jesus knew if the people received a revelation of why He came (to announce to the world who He was), then nothing could stop His kingdom from invading the heart of man throughout the earth. Indeed, when a man receives the revelation of Jesus, he will take the kingdom by force in his passion for the King. Matthew 11:12.

Keep in mind that Jesus told His audience then—and us today—to repent. Specifically, He told us to repent "because the kingdom is at hand." Notice that Jesus did not say, "repent because of your sins." Don't get me wrong—we do need to repent of the sin within us. But think about what "repent" means. It means to turn away. In saying, "Repent, for the kingdom of God is at hand," Jesus didn't focus on what we must turn away from. He focused on what we turn toward—His kingdom. The King and His culture. So Jesus says to repent because the King and His culture (His reign) are at hand. They are within grasp.

Jesus taught us to pray like this: "Our Father who is in Heaven, hallowed be Your name. Your kingdom come. Your will be done on earth as it is in heaven." Matthew 6:9-10. In other words, pray that the King and His culture would come on us as it is in heaven.

I believe Jesus gave us a prayer He fully expects to be answered today. That prayer is that His kingship and His heavenly culture will come to earth now. He taught us to pray for the Gospel to invade us. That His will would be done;

that His Kingdom would invade us so that the Gospel would not just be something we learn. Rather, Jesus desires that we become the Gospel. We do not just go and witness; we are a witness. Our mission is not just talking about the light; we are the light. Yes, we enter Jesus' kingdom through His death and resurrection—we cannot enter His kingdom without being saved. But we cannot be saved without first seeking His Kingdom. To seek His Kingdom is to hunger for a revelation of Him as King and of His culture.

C. Don't Miss the Author of the Good News

So often, mankind's salvation is presented as the core message of the Gospel. But as we've now seen from Scripture, it's actually the King and His culture. We must recognize this; otherwise, we've fallen into the trap of a partial conversation. Carried to its natural conclusion, this ends in vain conversation.

Why do I say that? Because when we only listen to the parts we perceive as good for us, that means we're ignoring the parts that don't appeal to us. That partial conversation eventually becomes a vain conversation—one that is futile. It doesn't bear good fruit. Rather than seek His Kingdom, we try to maintain our own kingdom—that is, we still try to be our own king living our own culture, hoping for an alliance with the King of kings, rather than allowing Jesus to be our King and our culture. And if we continue trying to be our own king or live our own culture, we've missed the Gospel.

Let's consider why that is. If we believe that the Gospel is only about man's salvation, we can miss the author of the benefits. For example, what if you owed a loan shark a million dollars, and were behind on your payments? You'd be pretty nervous, or at least you should be. Then, you hear that I am rich and love to get people out of debt. I'm guessing you would show up on my doorstep pretty quickly.

But why? Did you come because you want me? Or because you want what I have? If I paid your debt, would you have any lasting relationship with me? Or would you start drifting out of my life as soon as the check cleared? Or maybe you would hang around knowing you will need more of what I have later?

Would you tell people about me? You might tell people (especially those in debt) about my generosity. But would you tell them about me—who I am as a person? *Could* you tell them about me? How could you, if you never really got to know me?

Many people are told to come to Jesus because, through the work of the cross, He paid the price for their debt. I have no problem with people initially going to Jesus Christ because of what He can offer, so long as they come to accept that He is not just their Savior—He is their King and their culture. In reality, He does not save them until they seek His Kingdom.

But if people only go to Jesus because they hear He takes care of debt, what is the intention of their heart? Many have even re-cast the gospel of Christ as the "gospel of prosperity." This gospel centers on teachings that faith, positive speech, and monetary offerings will lead to increased material wealth.

While I do believe Christians can prosper, the focus on earthly wealth misses the point and, consequently, runs counter to the teachings of Jesus, who told us not to come to Him just to get what we want. After Jesus fed 5,000 men from five loaves and two fish, the crowd got in boats and followed Him all the way across the Sea of Galilee. John 6:1-25. That sounds good, right? They wanted to follow Jesus wherever He went. But Jesus knows the heart of man. He said to them, "You want to be with me because I fed you, not because you understood the miraculous signs." John 6:26 (NLT). In other words, Jesus tells them that He knew they didn't want to be with Him because they recognized who He is. They only wanted to be with Him because He filled their bellies. And if someone only wants Jesus because He can fill their belly, they are an enemy of the cross of Christ—it turns out their belly is really their god. Philippians 3:18-19.

Like Jesus, Paul distinguished between those who love Jesus for who He is and those who view Him as a path to wealth. Paul identifies those who "imagin[e] that godliness is a means of gain" as "depraved in mind and deprived of truth." 1 Timothy 6:5. Don't get me wrong, "godliness *with contentment* is great gain." 1 Timothy 6:6. But "those who desire to be rich fall into temptation, into a snare, into many senseless and harmful desires that plunge people into ruin and destruction." 1 Timothy 6:9. So it's hard to line up the prosperity gospel with the Gospel of the Kingdom. One looks to an earthly kingdom; the other looks to a Heavenly Kingdom. I fear that one also appeals to an earthly king (the hearer), while the other looks to a Heavenly King (the Creator).

Most people won't consciously think of Jesus like a get-rich-quick scheme. But many will still chase after God for all He has, can, and will do, without ever looking for Him. Think about this: what does Scripture call the miracles that Jesus performed? Signs and wonders. He intends the miracles to be signs pointing to Him. He intends that the miracles will cause us to wonder about Him. Sadly, many who heard Jesus' teaching fell in love with the signs and wonders themselves, without ever really seeing the One they pointed to.

The confusion stemming from this common misunderstanding that the Gospel is primarily about benefits for mankind can lead to a very wrong attitude toward the Provider of those benefits. I will put it bluntly. What would we call someone who is in a relationship just for the gifts that he or she receives from the other person? A gold digger. Jesus isn't looking for a gold-digging bride.

Each of us wants to be loved for who we are, not what we do. Who wants to be loved for their looks or their wealth or their athletic ability? All those things will pass. Beauty and athletic ability fade like a flower. 1 Peter 1:24. Wealth can be blown away in an instant. Haggai 1:9. Sure, we might use those things while we have them to get someone to look our way, but our heart cries out to be loved for who we are, not for what we have.

The same is true of God. He wants us to love Him for who He is, not for His abilities. He will use His resources to bless us, wooing us in the hope that we will look upon Him and fall in love with Him. Acts 14:17 ("He did not leave Himself without witness, in that He did good, gave us rain from heaven and fruitful seasons, filling our hearts with food and gladness."). But too many of us take the blessings without ever drawing close to Him. Instead, we use whatever blessings God sends into our lives to chase after idols—whether they're statues of silver and gold, shiny new cars, inappropriate relationships, or whatever else we covet. Jesus came to set us free from those idols, not to fund our pursuit of them.

I hope by now we can agree that God is looking for people who will acknowledge that we (mankind) are not the center of the Gospel. He is. The King. When we acknowledge and accept His reign over our lives, we get to take part in those benefits He graciously bestows on those who enter His Kingdom. But here's the strange thing about accepting Him as King: those benefits no longer become our main focus. They pale in comparison to His glory. Sure, He does amazing things for us who believe. But we will praise Him forever simply because of who He is.

Let me end this section with another question. If the Gospel is first and foremost about the King and His culture, then what's the Bible about? Let's now apply our new understanding of the Gospel to draw out the central theme of Scripture.

III.   The Greater Conversation

In the last chapter, we found that Scripture reveals that the Gospel (the Good News) is the Gospel of the Kingdom—the King and His culture. Now, let us take a look at how the King and His culture is the subject of the whole Bible.

We already talked about how the Gospel is frequently cast as being all about man's salvation. In reality, the subject of the Gospel is Jesus Christ. The result of receiving this revelation—and loving that the Gospel is all about Him— leads to salvation. We make the Gospel about us when we allow ourselves to get caught up in a partial conversation, listening only to the parts of the Bible that sound good to us. If we're not careful, that partial conversation can become a vain conversation—a conversation that bears no good fruit. And we don't want that, since John the Baptist said that "every tree which does not bear good fruit is cut down and thrown into the fire." Matthew 3:10. It is not God's desire (or our desire) that we fail to bear good fruit.

What's the antidote to a partial conversation? How can we keep what might have begun as a partial conversation from becoming a vain conversation? We can join the greater conversation—God's conversation. In the last chapter, I briefly described some of the key highlights described in the Bible: (1) creation; (2) the flood; (3) God's covenant with Abraham; (4) Moses and the Ten Commandments; (5) Jesus and the resurrection; (6) the birth of the New Testament church; and (7) Christ's return, which eventually leads to the fullness of heaven coming to earth, when God Himself will dwell with man. We're going to try to figure out the central theme that ties each of these together.

As we seek to understand the greater conversation, let's start with this question: who was before all time? Who existed before any of these events? Hopefully, that's an easy one for you—God! We know He existed before man; He made man. In fact, let's look at the very first verse of the Bible. It says, "In the beginning God created the heavens and the earth." Genesis 1:1. Who is being discussed? Who is the subject of this conversation? God.

What do you think occupied God's attention even before mankind's existence? I won't claim to know everything, but the Bible identifies at least two things.

First, the glory of God. In John 17, Jesus refers to "the glory that I had with you before the world existed." John 17:5 (ESV). Later in John 17, Jesus says that the Father loved him "before the foundation of the world." John 17:24 (ESV). What do you think it was like when there was no creation, just the uncreated Father, Son, and Holy Spirit, sharing love and glory?

Second, Jesus tells us that even before creating man, God prepared His kingdom. Matthew 25:34. What do you think this Kingdom is like? That's kind of a trick question. While Scripture gives us some glimpses, Paul said, "No eye has seen, nor ear heard, nor the heart of man imagined, what God has prepared for those who love him." 1 Corinthians 2:9 (ESV). You can't even imagine its goodness! God prepared this Kingdom for those who love Him. Who loves God most of all? My guess is Jesus, along with the Holy Spirit. But praise God that He gave me the grace to love Him, too—I'm looking forward to the fullness of His kingdom!

From these passages, we see that before man existed, the conversation was about God, His Glory, and His Kingdom. That's where the story started.

Fast forward now to the last part of the conversation currently available to us. Read Revelation 21 and 22, the last two chapters in the Bible, where the apostle John describes the vision he received of a new heaven and a new earth, where God will dwell with man. Do these chapters talk much about man? No. They are about God, His Kingdom, and His Glory. They talk of how the throne of God and the Lamb will rest in the New Jerusalem, evidencing God's reign over the Kingdom. Revelation 22:1. They also talk of the presence of God's glory in the New Jerusalem—in fact, the glory of God will shine so brightly in the city that it has no need of the sun or moon! Revelation 21:22-23.

So what does the beginning of the conversation focus on? God, His glory, and His kingdom. What does the end of the conversation focus on? God, His glory, and His kingdom.

Think about good books that you've read. If the introduction and conclusion of the book agree on one theme, does the middle of the book also follow that theme? Yes!

You've probably anticipated my next question. What do you think the entire Bible, including the plan of salvation, is about? Yes—God, His glory, and His kingdom! But I'm not asking you to take my word for it. Let's dig in to the greater conversation and see if I'm proclaiming the truth.

A.   In the Beginning

Even though the Bible begins at Genesis 1:1 and ends at Revelation 22:21, we know that the conversation did not start with Genesis and it does not end with Revelation. The beginning (that is, creation) is amazing, but I actually want to first look at what happened *before* the beginning. Wait—can something happen before the beginning? Maybe it's more accurate to say what happened outside the beginning. Thinking about it makes my head spin.

But that actually summarizes the point I want to make in this section. The awesome reality of God should make our heads spin. If it doesn't, the problem is with us, not Him. Before mankind was, God is. And so was His glory and His kingdom.

This may not be new information, but it is a powerful revelation. This type of revelation automatically changes our paradigm, helping us be more tuned into heavenly things and less tuned into worldly things. We are in the world, but we are not of the world. John 17:16.

That's easy to say, but harder to practice. Yet if we plant our minds in the permanence of God, His glory, and His kingdom, it will make it a lot easier for us to focus on that everlasting reality rather than the shiny, but temporary, things of this world.

1.   God was, and is, and is to come

The story starts with God. Period. God has no beginning and He has no end. Psalm 90:2. He is eternal.

Before creation was the Creator—"all things were made through Him, and without Him nothing was made that was made." John 1:3. He alone can say, "Surely My hand founded the earth, And My right hand spread out the heavens; when I call to them, they stand together." Isaiah 48:13. And, should we be arrogant enough to question Him, only He can say to us, like He said to Job, "Now prepare yourself like a man; I will question you, and you shall answer Me! Where were you when I laid the foundation of the earth?" Job 38:3-4.

Since God created time, God is not captured by time. Time is captured by the infinite Holy God! He is from everlasting to everlasting. Stop and just meditate on this great truth. God is not in a rush because He is, always has been, and always will be.

Being outside of time, God sees the end from the beginning. This gives Him a perspective we don't have. A thousand years to Him is like a day! 2 Peter 3:8. So, do not doubt God when it seems to you that He should act faster to resolve the chaos in the world today. 2 Peter 3:3-7. What we call delay is actually His patience, "not wishing that any should perish, but that all should reach repentance." 2 Peter 3:9 (ESV). Praise God for this! If He did not exercise this patience, He would have destroyed me long ago—long before I came to repentance.

The book of Genesis opens by affirming that God created the universe and its inhabitants, rather than the other way around: "In the beginning, God created the heavens and the earth." Genesis 1:1. John's gospel begins with the same words, but instead of focusing on creation, John focuses on Jesus: "In the beginning was the Word, and the Word was with God, and the Word was God." John 1:1. Jesus is the Word. John 1:14-15.

These first few verses of John's gospel show us that that the conversation started before Genesis 1:1, back when it was just Yahweh God. While God is one (Deuteronomy 6:4), the Father, the Son, and the Holy Spirit are distinct persons. We see a glimpse of those distinct persons in the very first verse of John. In that one verse, John tells us that the Word (which he later identifies as Jesus) "was God," yet also "was with God." Amazing! Later, we'll take a brief look at what we can glean from the Bible about the conversation between the Father and the Son before the world began.

2.   His eternal glory

We know that before creation, God was. He was glorious, even before creation was around to notice it (or to ignore it). As Jesus was about to go to the cross, He prayed to the Father, "O Father, glorify Me together with Yourself, with the glory which I had with You before the world was." John 17:5. We see here that Jesus and the Father had glory together before the creation of the world.

What is "glory"? It refers to God's infinite, intrinsic worth, or splendor.[6] His splendor is infinite—it has no limits. And His splendor is intrinsic, meaning it is His very nature. And so, like God, His glory existed before creation because it is His very nature.

The Greek word (*doxa*) translated as "glory" in the New Testament corresponds to a Hebrew word translated as "glory" in the Old Testament. That Hebrew word (*kabo*) also means "to be heavy." I think this gives us such a powerful image. God's splendor is heavy—it is palpable.

We see this in the Old Testament, when "the LORD descended in the cloud and stood with [Moses] there, and proclaimed the name of the LORD." Exodus 34:5. When Moses descended from the mountain, the skin of his face shone. Exodus 34:30. The glory of God was so heavy, so palpable, that Moses glowed even after he left the presence of the Lord.

---

[6] HELPS Word-studies, Helps Ministries, Inc. (available at http://biblehub.com/greek/1391.htm).

God's glory is beyond our ability to obtain or handle. It is beyond our grasp. In fact, when Moses came down from the mountain, "the children of Israel could not look steadily at [his] face . . . because of the glory of his countenance." 2 Corinthians 3:13. So Moses put a veil over his face, and the children of Israel hid from the glory.

That may sound weird to us, but Paul says the very same thing happens today. He says that if the "gospel is veiled, it is veiled to those who are perishing, whose minds the god of this age has blinded, who do not believe, lest the light of the gospel of the glory of Christ, who is the image of God, should shine on them." 2 Corinthians 4:3-4. So those who don't believe are blind to the Good News of the infinite, intrinsic splendor of Jesus. They have no concept of His worth.

But we believers know that Jesus is the very "radiance of the glory of God." Hebrews 1:3. And Jesus desires that we who believe would see His glory that the Father gave Him. John 17:24. He is the glorious One, full of beauty. But the lost—those who are perishing—just can't see it. For them, the Good News of the glory of Christ is hidden behind a veil. Church, does that break our heart? If we love what He loves and hate what He hates, it will.

We could talk a lot more about God's glory, but for now, let's agree that God is glorious, and that He possessed that glory before man existed.

3.   His Kingdom

God prepared a kingdom before the foundation of the world. Matthew 25:34. We talked in Chapter 2 about how the word "kingdom" can be thought of as the king and his culture.

That also applies to the Greek word *basileian*, the word

translated as "kingdom" in this verse. The underlying word *basileia* means, in a physical sense, the king's realm and, in the abstract sense, his rule.[7] Or stated differently, the "kingdom" includes not just God's physical kingdom, but also his style of rule—His culture.

So, in Matthew 25, we hear from Jesus that, before man, there was a Kingdom. And not any kingdom, but one with the greatest King sitting on the throne. One with perfect dominion over His domain. His title is King of kings!

So before mankind, there was God, His Glory, and His Kingdom. As we will see, the conversation remains centered on God, His Glory, and His Kingdom throughout the Bible.

---

[7] HELPS Word-studies, Helps Ministries, Inc. (1987, 2011) (available at http://biblehub.com/greek/932.htm).

B.   Two Kingdoms: A Greater and a Lesser

We read above that, "In the beginning, God created the heavens and the earth." Genesis 1:1. Isaiah tells us that He "did not create it in vain"; He "formed it to be inhabited." Isaiah 45:18. And indeed God Himself spoke to the Israelites that, "In six days, the Lord made the heavens and the earth, the sea, and all that is in them." Exodus 20:11. On completion, God approved of His handiwork: "Then God saw everything that He had made, and indeed it was very good." Genesis 1:31.

We know that the Kingdom included not just Adam, Eve, and the animals. It also included heavenly beings—a lot of them. In Revelation, John sees angels surrounding the throne of God, describing the number as "ten thousand times ten thousand, and thousands of thousands." Revelation 5:11.

Once upon a time, the Kingdom of God was full of peace and one accord. All were united under one Kingdom—one King and one culture. Only God Most High had dominion over the domain. All gave glory to the God who was, and is, and is to come, the Alpha and Omega.

But things didn't stay that way. One of those heavenly beings, called Lucifer (or "shining one"), rebelled against the King. Understand that this wasn't because he was low in position. To the contrary, Scripture describes him as "the seal of perfection, full of wisdom and perfect in beauty," covered in "every precious stone." Ezekiel 28:12-13. He possessed not only beauty and wisdom, but also high position. He was "the anointed cherub who covers." Some understand this to mean that his wings covered the very throne of God.

Yet for all that, he was not satisfied. He let the beauty that God bestowed upon him corrupt him. His "heart was lifted up because of [his] beauty"; he "corrupted [his] wisdom for the sake of [his] splendor." Ezekiel 28:17. The sin rose in his heart.

Isaiah describes the result of Lucifer's sin: "How you are fallen from heaven, O Lucifer, son of the morning!" Isaiah 14:12. No longer was he the anointed cherub who covers. Lucifer's sin was not a surprise to the all-knowing God, but it nevertheless was a great tragedy—the effects of which you and I still suffer to this day, and will until the return of the Lord.

Let's look closer at Lucifer's sin. Five times, Lucifer says in his heart, "I Will":

- I Will ascend into heaven;

- I Will exalt my throne above the stars of God;

- I Will sit also upon the mount of the congregation;

- I Will ascend above the heights of the clouds; and

- I Will be like the Most High.

Isaiah 14:13-14.

Lucifer no longer wanted to give God glory, nor did he want God to have dominion over him. He wanted his own kingdom. He wanted to be king. Lucifer thought that if he sat on the throne, that would make him *the* king. But it does not. We know that a throne is handed down through the royal bloodline, something Lucifer could not claim. So he wanted something that he could never be—at least not without a war.

Lucifer is the first to commit treason (that is, the crime of betraying one's sovereign authority). God dismissed Lucifer from his high position because Lucifer wanted the throne. Not because he did drugs, had sex outside of marriage, stole, murdered, or anything else. Lucifer no longer wanted the will of God, but his own "I will." Lucifer's "I wills" were the reason he could no longer serve as the anointed cherub of God, the Glorious One.

If Lucifer became Satan (which means "Adversary" or "Accuser") and lost his position in heaven because he elevated his will above God's will, is it possible that salvation may be more than being forgiven? Is it possible that salvation is not just a prayer? Could it also be about letting go of our will and entering into His will? Hold on to that question as we move further into the story.

When Lucifer declared his will to sit on the throne and to be like the Most High, no longer was all creation united in obedience to God. There was now a pretender to the throne. Lucifer, the anointed cherub, became Satan, the adversary of God, the accuser of the brethren.

1.   Mankind falls for a partial truth

Like all would-be kings, Satan sought a following. He sought followers who would exalt him like he desired. Jesus said that the "kings of the Gentiles exercise lordship over them" (Luke 22:25), meaning the Gentile kings were domineering, ruling for shameful gain (1 Peter 5:3). This is the type of ruler Satan wants to be, in contrast to Jesus, who rules with the scepter of righteousness. Hebrews 1:8.

But Satan is the subtlest of all creatures. Genesis 3:1; Revelation 12:9. In implementing his plan to build a following, he did not show up and say, "Worship me instead of God Most High." Satan is "a liar and the father of lies." John 8:44. More specifically, he is "the deceiver of the whole world." Revelation 12:9. Even more specifically, he deceives us with partial truth.

A partial truth is different than a partial conversation. As a brief reminder, when we talk about a partial conversation, we're focusing on the person who is joining a conversation in progress. For example, a person sitting next to two people having a conversation might overhear something he likes, prompting him to join the conversation.

The problem is that he's only heard the part that interests him—he didn't hear the full truth, only the facts that were music to his ears. And he doesn't bother to obtain an accurate understanding of the whole conversation before leaping in. He fills in the factual gaps with assumptions, then leaps to a logical, albeit often wrong, conclusion.

This tendency to jump into partial conversation based on pleasant facts rather than the full truth goes back to the appetite for facts (rather than truth) that mankind acquired in the Garden of Eden, when Adam and Eve ate the fruit from the tree of knowledge of good and evil. They only liked the idea that the fruit could make them wise (that is, acquiring facts), but this temptation led them to overlook the truth that "the fear of the Lord is the beginning of wisdom, and the knowledge of the Holy One is understanding." Proverbs 9:10.

Since a partial conversation occurs when a person overhearing the conversation joins without bothering to understand the whole conversation, it can occur without any deceptive intent by the original parties to the conversation. But a partial truth is different—the person speaking a partial truth does so in a deliberate effort to deceive his audience. He selectively gives you some (true) facts in an effort to create a wrong impression. He hopes you won't make the effort to learn the rest of the facts necessary to understand the truth. So when a person receives a partial truth, it tends to prevent him from hearing the full truth. The end result: believing a lie.

Here's an example. Imagine you're looking for your first house. You come across a brand-new neighborhood that's just under development. The salesperson has beautiful drawings showing what the neighborhood will look like when finished, with an awesome swimming pool, clubhouse, and tennis courts. None of this exists now, but the salesperson assures you that construction on those amenities will start soon . . . she just can't guarantee when. But by buying now, you get the house for a lower price than when the pool and all the other extras are finished.

This all sounds great to you! So great that you don't listen to that small voice in your head asking, "But what if they never start building the amenities?" You don't bother to figure out the developer is already on the brink of financial collapse and has no money to build the amenities. The deception was based on truth—the developer really did plan to build all those amenities. But it was deception because the developer withheld the rest of the story—that the plan was already failing.

Like the deceptive developer, Satan tactically uses facts that appeal to the target of his deception in trying to develop his rule and authority. In leading someone away from the Truth (Jesus), the best partial truth focuses exclusively on comfort, salvation, or pleasure to the individual. Why? Since our flesh desires those things, those are what we like to hear about. Satan knows that a man caught up in his own interest will not devote himself to what interests God. "For the desires of the flesh are against the Spirit, and the desires of the Spirit are against the flesh, for these are opposed to each other, to keep you from doing the things that you want to do." Galatians 5:17.

History's first recorded use of partial truth comes in Genesis 3. God had told Adam not to eat of the fruit of the Tree of Knowledge of Good and Evil, or he would surely die. Genesis 2:17. The serpent convinced Eve, using deception, to eat of the fruit of the Tree of Knowledge of Good and Evil.

He did this by mingling truth with a lie. He told her that if she ate the fruit, "You will not surely die. For God knows that in the day you eat of it your eyes will be opened, and you will be like God." Genesis 3:4-5. It was a lie that she would not die. But, as strange as it sounds, it was true in a sense that she would be like God. After they ate, God said, "'Behold, the man has become like one of Us, to know good and evil." Genesis 3:22-23. Of course, this didn't work out like she probably expected.

While Eve was deceived, I want to emphasize something: the mere fact that Eve was deceived does not justify her rebellion. She was deceived because she was only listening for her own gain; she was not focused on her Creator. She tried to use that as an excuse, just like I probably would have done, but it didn't work. Genesis 3:13. Both Adam and Eve walked away from God to fulfill their desire. And, as God promised, they surely died.[8]

Dying wasn't the only consequence of Adam and Eve's sin. Remember that God had given Adam and Eve dominion. God told them, "Fill the earth and subdue it; have dominion

---

[8] People often ask why Adam did not physically die for more than 900 years after eating the fruit, since God said, "in the day you eat of it you shall surely die." Genesis 2:17. This is a great question. People often say that this verse refers to spiritual death (that is, being cut off from God). And while that's true, this verse does also talk about physical death, and it was fulfilled just as God spoke it.

To understand how God's warning in Genesis 2:17 was fulfilled by Adam and Eve's physical death, it's helpful to take a look at the literal phrasing in Hebrew, the original language of Genesis. As the New King James Version indicates in a footnote, the Hebrew more literally says, "dying you shall die." This captures what happened to Adam and Eve very precisely. We know that Adam's sin put creation in bondage to decay. Romans 8:21 (NIV). Once they sinned, Adam and Eve were in decay towards death. So, like the Bible says, dying they surely died. *See* "The spiritual death of the Adam tribe?" Creation Ministries, Jan. 12, 2014, accessed Nov. 16, 2016, http://creation.com/adam-tribe.

over the fish of the sea, over the birds of the air, and over every living thing that moves on the earth." Genesis 1:28. What happened in their domain as a result of sin? That domain rebelled against them. God cursed the ground to bring forth thistle and thorn against man's effort to cultivate food, while living creatures became a threat to shed man's blood. Genesis 3:17-19; Genesis 9:5-6.

Looking at Adam's pre-sin dominion versus the state of affairs after his sin might prompt you to ask why Adam disobeyed God in the first place. We know it wasn't because he was deceived—Scripture says that only Eve was deceived. 1 Timothy 2:14. Adam ate willingly and willfully. Then why did he eat? While I'm sure he agreed with Eve that the fruit of the Tree of Knowledge of Good and Evil was pleasant to the sight, I don't think that was the main draw. I think Adam wanted to be like God. Not just in the sense of knowing good and evil, but being truly sovereign.

If Adam was shooting for sovereignty, he failed. Miserably. It wasn't just that Adam now had to struggle against the very creation over which he'd received dominion. It was worse than that. Satan came to be "the ruler of this world" (John 12:31; 14:30), gaining his own "domain of darkness." Colossians 1:13. Jesus even said that Satan possesses a kingdom. Luke 11:18; Matthew 12:26.

While Jesus referred to Satan as having a kingdom, notice that He didn't refer to Satan as a king. Jesus elsewhere referred to Satan as "the ruler of this world," using the Greek word *archon*. John 12:31, 14:30. Paul used a related word, *archonta*, in Ephesians 2, in a phrase that can be translated "prince of the power of the air." Ephesians 2:2. While the Greek word *archon* denotes significant authority (for example, ruler, governor, prince, or magistrate), it is not generally translated as "king."[9]

Why might it be that Jesus referred to the kingdom of Satan without referring to him as a king? Remember our earlier discussion about kings. See Section II(B)(1). A king becomes king by right of inheritance—because of who he is. That description doesn't fit Satan. He isn't king by inheritance or birthright; he is a pretender to the throne of God. It does describe Jesus, the One of whom God said, "You are My Son; today I have begotten You. Ask of Me, and I will give You the nations for Your inheritance, and the ends of the earth for Your possession." Psalm 2:7-8.

While Jesus referred to Satan's kingdom, notice that He did so only in explaining that Satan's kingdom could not stand against the kingdom of God: "When a strong man, fully armed, guards his own palace, his goods are in peace. But when a stronger than he comes upon him and overcomes him, he takes from him all his armor in which he trusted, and divides his spoils." Luke 11:21-22. Think of Satan as the strong man, fully armed. His goods are safe until "a stronger than he," that is, Jesus, comes along. The strong man cannot stand against the One stronger than He, and he loses his possessions.

Maybe this lesser status is why Paul chose not to refer to Satan's "kingdom" in Colossians 1, but instead to Satan's "domain." The Greek word translated "domain" is *exousia*. It comes from two root words generally meaning "out from" and "authority."[10] So *exousia* refers to an authority coming out from some other source. That's what Satan has—he has authority, but unlike a king, it's not because of who he is. Satan only has the authority granted him by God.

We see this play out in Luke 4, where Satan, while

---

[9] HELPS Word-studies, Helps Ministries, Inc. (1987, 2011) (available at http://biblehub.com/greek/758.htm).

[10] HELPS Word-studies, Helps Ministries, Inc. (1987, 2011) (available at http://biblehub.com/greek/1849.htm).

tempting Jesus in the wilderness, showed Him "all the kingdoms of the world." Satan says, "This has been delivered to me, and I give it to whomever I wish." Luke 4:5-6. While we shouldn't put much stock in what Satan says, Jesus didn't disagree with his statement. In fact, Jesus elsewhere referred to "Satan's throne." Revelation 2:13. But Jesus did trump Satan's authority over the kingdoms of the world by pointing to the King of kings, "You shall worship the LORD your God, and Him only you shall serve." Luke 4:8.

So, while we may refer to Satan's kingdom, it's with the understanding that any authority Satan currently has derives from, and is subservient to, God's sovereignty. In other words, Satan is not on equal footing with God. God is "the blessed and only Sovereign, the King of kings and Lord of lords." 1 Timothy 6:15 (ESV). "Know this day, and consider it in your heart, that the LORD Himself is God in heaven above and on the earth beneath; there is no other." Deuteronomy 4:39. God says, "Heaven is My throne, and earth is My footstool." Acts 7:49. So what Satan considers his kingdom (this world), God considers His footstool.

What does that tell us about God's sovereignty versus Satan's authority? It tells us, "Whatever the LORD pleases, He does, in heaven and in earth, in the seas and in all deeps." Psalm 135:6. And it pleased the Father to "give all authority in heaven and on earth to Jesus." Matthew 28:18. In His hand "are power and might, so that none is able to withstand [Him]." 2 Chronicles 20:6. Therefore, it's not surprising that every time we see a head-to-head matchup between Jesus and Satan in the Bible, Jesus wins—no contest! Revelation 19:11-20:3; Revelation 20:7-10.

But at the same time, we have to understand that Satan's throne, power, and great authority are a current reality. Revelation 13:2. God reigns supreme over all creation, but for that very reason He can give authority to whomever He wants. He says, "I have made the earth, the man and the beast that are on the ground, by My great power and by My outstretched arm, and have given it to whom it seemed proper to Me." Jeremiah 27:4-5. In that context, He was explaining that He would allow King Nebuchadnezzar of Babylon authority over Israel and the surrounding nations. In a similar way, God allows Satan a measure of authority within His creation. Satan has a domain. Remember that a domain refers not just to physical rule, but also to culture. Satan's kingdom operates according to Satan's culture. And Satan's culture operates in rebellion against God's reign.

You may be asking yourself, "But why, Lord?"—a good question. God doesn't force people to enter His Kingdom—He wants us to enter it willingly. Until we seek His Kingdom, God allows us to live in Satan's kingdom (that is, under his authority). As you've probably realized, the culture of Satan's kingdom is not like Jesus' culture. The culture of Jesus' kingdom is this: "Not my will, but my Father's will be done." The culture of Satan's kingdom is: "Do as thou wilt." Be your own man, god, King! The fruit of Jesus' culture is life and life abundantly. We get this life abundantly when we lose our life so we can gain life, His Life. The fruit of Satan's culture is death and death universally. The way death comes is by us trying to save our lives, wills, and kingdoms. "Whoever tries to save his life will lose it, but whoever loses his life will preserve it." Luke 17:33 (NIV).

How do we feel about Satan's culture? Do we hate its evil, especially our own evil? Do we hate it enough to forsake everything we have in Satan's kingdom to cross over to God's kingdom? Or do we love the darkness of Satan's kingdom, seeing it as cover for the evil deeds we love to practice? Do we love the lie that we can be our own king? Is our lust to be our own man or woman so strong that we would rather continue to feed our flesh's desires? God grants us this time in Satan's kingdom to make that decision. Because no one who loves that lie will enter God's Kingdom. Revelation 22:15.

2.   Satan's kingdom expands

After Adam brought sin into the world, Satan's kingdom expanded as mankind expanded. With mankind brought into bondage to sin, creation was placed in "bondage to corruption." John 8:34; Romans 8:21. Proverbs speaks to this, saying that "the earth trembles" over "a servant when he reigns." Proverbs 30:21-22. That's exactly what happened. Satan was created a servant of God, yet he became ruler of this world, and the earth trembles to this day.

Mankind did not escape the bondage to corruption. It didn't take long for Satan's culture to bear its bad fruit. Cain killed Abel and it went downhill from there. In a little more than 1,500 years, "the Lord saw that the wickedness of man was great in the earth, and that every intent of the thoughts of his heart was only evil continually." Gen. 6:5. Praise God that "Noah found grace in the eyes of the Lord" (Gen. 5:8), or I wouldn't have written this book and you wouldn't be reading it!

But unfortunately, man's evil heart did not end with the flood: "the heart is deceitful above all things, and desperately sick. Who can understand it?" Jeremiah 17:9. The flood destroyed the world, but it did not restore the world. Scripture is clear that all have sinned and fall short of the glory of God." Romans 3:23. As King David wrote, "Surely I was sinful at birth, sinful from the time my mother conceived me." Psalm 51:5 (NIV).

Every single one of us has been a citizen under Satan's jurisdiction. Everyone has practiced his culture and followed his motto—"I will." In the book of Ephesians, Paul reminds believers that even they were once (emphasis on the "once") "dead in the trespasses and sins in which you once walked, following the course of this world, following the prince of the power of the air." Ephesians 2:1-2. He says we "were by nature children of wrath, like the rest of mankind." Ephesians 2:3.

Sometimes people like to think of themselves as sitting on the fence between God's kingdom and Satan's. But in truth, everyone is in one or the other. When Jesus referred to Satan's kingdom, it came in response to the Pharisees accusing Jesus of casting out demons by the power of "the prince of demons." Luke 11:15. Jesus first pointed out the illogic of their accusation, asking, "If Satan also is divided against himself, how will his kingdom stand?" Luke 11:18. But then look at what Jesus says: "If it is by the finger of God that I cast out demons, then the kingdom of God has come upon you." Luke 11:20.

Notice that Jesus didn't just say that the Kingdom of God had come upon Satan. He said, "the kingdom of God has come upon *you*," speaking to his accusers. They were in Satan's kingdom, underneath his jurisdiction, so the Kingdom of God was coming upon them too. Jesus brought this point home by following up with this: "Whoever is not with me is against me." Luke 11:23. No one has always been with Jesus. People who think they are "on the fence" ensure that Satan's kingdom remains crowded.

The bad news is that Satan's kingdom expands by birth—every man born of flesh is born into Satan's jurisdiction. But the good news is that God's Kingdom also expands by birth—and it's expanding all the time: "Most assuredly, I say to you, unless one is born again, he cannot see the kingdom of God." John 3:3. When someone is "born, not of blood nor of the will of man, but of God" (John 1:13), Satan has no power to stop the loss to his kingdom. He's the strong man whose possessions are stripped by "a stronger than he." Luke

11:21-22. And not only do those born of God become citizens of God's Kingdom, "to them He gave the right to become children of God." John 1:12-13.

C.   God's Plan for Salvation

God is not surprised by my sin or your sin. He declares the end from the beginning, and everything in between. And that declaration includes the plan of salvation. It was His will.

Remember that the story began with God, His Glory, and His Kingdom. That remains true even of the plan of salvation. The cross is all about God, His Glory, and His Kingdom.

The cross is about God—just consider the One who went to the cross. John the apostle began his gospel with these famous words: "In the beginning was the Word, and the Word was with God, and the Word was God." John 1:1-2. He then identifies Jesus as the Word, saying "the Word became flesh and dwelt among us." John 1:14. John then records the words of another John, John the Baptist, who saw the Holy Spirit descend and remain on Jesus: "I have seen and testified that this is the Son of God." John 1:34. If that isn't good enough, after Jesus was baptized by John the Baptist and the Spirit alighted on Him, "a voice came from heaven, saying, 'This is my beloved Son, in whom I am well pleased.'" Matthew 3:17.

Since Jesus came, a long line of people have denied that He is the Christ, the Son of the living God. John didn't mince words in describing these folks: "Who is the liar but he who denies that Jesus is the Christ? This is the antichrist, he who denies the Father and the Son." 1 John 2:22-23.

The cross is about His Kingdom (don't worry, I'm not forgetting His glory—I'll come back to it in a minute). I hope I'm not spoiling the story for you by saying that Jesus' sacrifice was necessary for our salvation. But remember that salvation is not spiritually stationary. We change kingdoms, leaving slavery under Satan's rule to become children of God under the rule of His Son. Paul tells us in Colossians that God "has delivered us from the domain of darkness and transferred us to the kingdom of His beloved Son." Colossians 1:13 (ESV). And once we are transferred into that Kingdom, we become citizens—Paul tells us in Philippians that "our citizenship is in heaven." Philippians 3:20. We are not trespassers; we belong! So we see that salvation is indeed about His Kingdom.

The cross is also about God's glory—His infinite, intrinsic value. Let's explore how God is glorified through man's salvation.

In Isaiah, God tells Israel, "I have formed him, yes, I have made him." Who is He talking about? "Everyone who is called by My name." Isaiah 43:7. It is not just Israel that is called by His name, since "the salvation of God has [also] been sent to the Gentiles." Acts 28:28. Peter says, "If anyone suffers as a Christian, let him not be ashamed, but let him glorify God in that name." 1 Peter 4:16 (ESV). We who believe in Christ are called by His name.

And that takes us back to Isaiah, where God says that those who are "called by My name . . . I have created for My glory." Isaiah 43:7. Did you get that? He created us—those who are called by His name—for His glory!

The cross was necessary for God to take glory in us, because "all have sinned and fall short of the glory of God." Romans 3:23. When we were lost in our sins, what glory could He take in us? Paul tells us that "the carnal mind is enmity against God." Romans 8:7. In fact, "those who are in the flesh cannot please God." Romans 8:8.

That's a big problem, right? We can't do anything on our own to get right with God. Paul tells us that "by the deeds of the law no flesh will be justified in His sight." Romans 3:20.

Our salvation will not come of our "own works, lest anyone should boast." Ephesians 2:9. So who "will deliver [us] from this body of death?" Romans 7:24. Jesus Christ! "The Lamb of God who takes away the sin of the world." John 1:29.

It's important that we understand something here. We often say that salvation is a gift, and so it is: "For by grace you have been saved through faith . . . it is the gift of God, not of works, lest anyone should boast." Ephesians 2:8. But that doesn't mean it was without cost. When you give someone a birthday present, it doesn't cost the birthday boy or girl anything. But that doesn't mean that it was free to you, the giver of the gift. In fact, that's what makes a gift special. You sacrificed something to give the gift.

That is certainly true of the salvation from sin that God provides to all who believe in the name of the only Son of God (John 3:16-18)—the price that was paid is incredible. We were "not redeemed with corruptible things like silver or gold . . . but with the precious blood of Christ, as of a lamb without blemish and without spot." 1 Peter 1:18-19. Earlier, we talked about the glory, the intrinsic value, of Christ. How precious then His blood, which was shed for our sin! So, while God gives salvation as a gift, we can never forget that our redemption from sin came with an awesome price. We just weren't the ones who paid it.

With that background, let's look briefly at a few examples demonstrating that salvation remains about God's glory.

1. Jesus' glorified the Father by working out the plan for salvation

You fathers out there will join me in testifying that a father is glorified when his children are obedient. This is true even when we're talking about small things, like cleaning up their dishes without being told. But how much more so when they are obedient in bigger things, like maybe when your college-aged kid chooses to go on a mission trip for spring break instead of the beach.

With these small, earthly examples in mind, try to imagine how the Father was glorified in Jesus as He chose to lay down His life to carry out the plan of salvation. Let's consider what this entailed.

a)   Doing the Father's will

The Son of God existed with the Father in heaven before the foundation of the world. And He had glory with the Father before the world was. John 17:5. Yet He left that glory with the Father to become flesh and dwell among us. John 1:14. Why? In exploring the question why Jesus left the glory He had with the Father to dwell among us, let me start by asking a different question: Do you think the Father and the Son were having a conversation with each other before creating the heavens and earth? You bet! I can't wait to learn more about that conversation, but Scripture gives us a few glimpses of their interaction—and these glimpses tell us a little about why Jesus put on flesh and dwelt among us 2,000 years ago.

Jesus says that the Father loved Him "before the foundation of the world." John 17:24. That may not surprise you. But Scripture also tells us that Jesus' sacrificial offering as the Lamb without blemish or spot was "foreknown before the foundation of the world." 1 Peter 1:18-20.

Why was Jesus' sacrifice known before the world was created? Because God also promised the "hope of eternal life . . . before the beginning of time." Titus 1:2 (NIV). Who was promised eternal life before time? Us! God "chose us in Him before the foundation of the world." Ephesians 1:4.

This might prompt you to ask, "But didn't God know we would sin?" Of course! He "declar[es] the end from the beginning." Isaiah 46:10. He "chose us in Him" despite foreseeing all our sin. He knew eternal life would not come because of anything we have done, but by His grace (that is, His unmerited favor). And "this grace was given us in Christ Jesus before the beginning of time." 2 Tim. 1:9.

So, even before time began, our salvation was "the purpose of [the Father's] will." Ephesians 1:5. But not only was eternal life the Father's will, it was also His promise. Titus 1:2. But who was listening when the Father made that promise, since the saints weren't around to hear it? Jesus! The Father "chose us in Him before the foundation of the world" (Eph. 1:4), and gave us to Jesus (John 17:9, 20).

Why was our salvation the Father's will? Why did He promise us to Jesus? Many people say God created us to be in relationship with Him. I think that's true, but it's pretty vague. What does that mean?

The Bible tells us about the relationship God wants with us. The Bible says that believers, individually, "are children of God." 1 John 3:2. And it says that believers, collectively, are the bride of Christ. Ephesians 5:31-32; Romans 7:4. These are the relationships God created us for.

In the Song of Solomon, the bride's beloved refers to her as "my sister, my spouse." Song of Solomon 4:9. We understand the Song of Solomon as referring not only to earthly marriage, but also to the heavenly marriage between Christ (the bride's beloved) and His bride. The phrase "my sister, my spouse" captures our relationship to God so beautifully. As the Father's adopted children, the body of Christ (collectively) is Jesus' sister. And we are also His bride, His spouse.

But that bride had to be redeemed. That was the Father's will before the foundation of the world. That brings us to how Jesus glorified the Father in doing His will.

b)   Jesus: obedient unto death

Step back and think about just what it meant for the Son of God to leave the glory He had with the Father in heaven and descend to earth to take on flesh. In Hebrews, we read that Jesus "for a little while was made lower than the angels . . . so that by the grace of God he might taste death for everyone." Hebrews 2:9 (ESV).

In heaven, the Son of God received worship from angels. Yet, for a while, He was made lower than the angels. And while He came to proclaim the Kingdom, He didn't appear fully formed in kingly glory. No, He arrived as an embryo. So insignificant in the eyes of the world that, in America alone, we suck 1 million of them out of a mother's womb every year.

And nine or so months later, He was born of a woman, a baby laid in a manger. Luke 2:7. I'm sure Mary was an awesome mom, but imagine the Son of God having to wait on a poor young woman to—at her convenience—feed Him and change His diaper (or whatever they used back then)! Fast forward through the inevitable teasing of younger children, awkwardness of adolescence, working for a living as a carpenter even though He owned all things, and all the other things we would never, with our fleshly minds, expect the King of kings to submit Himself to.

When we consider all that, is it surprising that the Bible says, "though [Jesus] was a Son, yet He learned obedience by the things which He suffered"? Hebrews 5:8. The concept of Jesus learning obedience may sound weird if you haven't explored it before, but Scripture is explicit. Paul makes the same point in Philippians, saying, "being found in appearance as a man, He humbled Himself and became obedient to the point of death, even the death of the cross." Philippians 2:8.

Don't get me wrong. I'm not saying Jesus was a disobedient Son when He was with the Father in heaven before coming in the flesh. But in humbling Himself—even unto death—He had an opportunity to exercise obedience in a way that maybe He hadn't in the glory He had with the Father. Think of it like this: if your will always perfectly aligned with God's will, would you really know obedience? Or would you learn obedience only when your will did not align with the Father's, forcing you to choose whose will to follow?

For Jesus, this question came into sharp focus after the last supper, when Jesus—knowing very clearly what was to come—told His disciples, "My soul is exceedingly sorrowful, even to death." Matthew 26:38. As Jesus prayed to the Father, He said, "O My Father, if it is possible, let this cup pass from Me; nevertheless, not as I will, but as You will." Matthew 26:39. In other words, if there was a way for Jesus to accomplish His mission without the cross, He was asking for that alternate route.

While the Father provided an angel from heaven to strengthen Jesus (Luke 22:43), that assistance did not take away the sorrow at the coming wrath of God that Jesus was to endure for our sake. Rather, it gave Jesus strength to carry out His mission. Scripture confirms that Jesus remained in agony—"His sweat became like great drops of blood falling down to the ground." Yet He didn't turn away from God; He "prayed more earnestly." Luke 22:44. Jesus did not waver in His resolve to do the Father's will. He prayed a second time, and then a third, saying, "O My Father, if this cup cannot pass away from Me unless I drink it, Your will be done." Matthew 26:42-44.

How true, then, were Paul's words when he said that Jesus "humbled Himself and became obedient to the point of death, even the death of the cross." Philippians 2:8. It's not as though Jesus didn't have options. Jesus Himself said to those who arrested him, "Do you think that I cannot now pray to My Father, and He will provide Me with more than twelve legions of angels?" Matthew 26:53. Jesus could have hit the eject button any time He chose. But that wasn't the Father's will. What obedience!

I started this section by asking if fathers would agree that we are glorified by our children's obedience. After this brief look at the ultimate obedience Jesus showed in carrying out the Father's will, how could we reach any conclusion except that Jesus' work on the cross brought God glory? Hopefully, that's obvious to us, but if not, Scripture confirms it.

In John 17, the apostle John records Jesus' prayer to the Father just before He enters the garden where Judas betrays Him. This intense prayer gives us an incredible glimpse of the conversation between the Father and the Son that has been going on since before the world was. If you haven't studied this chapter, I highly recommend you do so. While Jesus packs many amazing things in these 26 verses, I'm only going to focus on glory here. Glory is a frequent topic in this prayer.

Jesus says to His Father, "I have glorified You on the earth. I have finished the work which You have given Me to do." John 17:4. Earlier, I said that "glory" refers to infinite, inherent value. So, it follows that to "glorify" God is to personally recognize His infinite, inherent value. Jesus says that's what He did in doing the Father's work—Jesus recognized the Father's infinite, inherent value by acting in obedience to the Father.

Jesus also received glory from the Father through His

work on the cross. Jesus said, "And now, O Father, glorify Me together with Yourself, with the glory which I had with You before the world was." John 17:5. As an aside, it's interesting that Jesus included this request in His prayer to the Father in John 17. Earlier, at the last supper, Jesus had said that the Father would indeed glorify Him: "Now the Son of Man is glorified, and God is glorified in Him. If God is glorified in Him, God will also glorify Him in Himself, and glorify Him immediately." John 13:31-32.

Since we know that Jesus only spoke what the Father told Him (John 5:19), Jesus knew that the Father would indeed glorify Him. So why did He make that request in John 17? Jesus was repeating the Father's promises back to the Father, praying the Father's word to the Father. This is a good lesson for us who desire to abide in His word, in His promises. And, as always, the Father was faithful to His Word. In Hebrews 2, it says that Jesus was "crowned with glory and honor because of the suffering of death." Hebrews 2:9.

To sum this up, Jesus was able and empowered to fulfill His Father's will because He was interested in, and invested in, the larger conversation. Satan tried to lure Jesus into a partial conversation by offering Him instant gratification with a partial truth—saying he would give Jesus the kingdoms of the world if Jesus would worship him. This was a partial truth because Satan was offering a counterfeit version of what the Father was offering. And it would result in a partial conversation because it would result in Jesus seeking instant personal glory, rather than giving glory to the Father. Jesus could withstand that temptation because He didn't have ears just for the part of the conversation that appealed to Him.

Jesus' obedience brought glory. The Father received glory through His Son's obedience in taking on flesh and dwelling among us. The Father received glory in the Son's obedience even unto death. And the Son, in exercising His obedience to the Father, received glory from the Father. What a beautiful picture into the relationship between Father and Son!

2.   The Father's glory in His adopted children

When we consider the benefits of salvation, it's easy for us to focus solely on the benefits to us. And indeed they are amazing. We who once were at enmity with God now "have peace with God through our Lord Jesus Christ." Romans 5:1. Hallelujah! But it's way more than that—we also "receive[] the Spirit of adoption by whom we cry out, 'Abba [Papa], Father." Romans 8:15. We become children of the Creator God!

This is so incredible that it's hard to avoid thinking about it only from our perspective. But let's not forget that God is the subject of this conversation. So let's ask the question—how does our salvation bring God glory? Here's the answer: after we are reconciled to God (and only after), He can take glory in us.

That may make you squirm a bit as you think of your unsaved friends and family members. It should. This is a matter of (eternal) life and death. Unless you're born of God, you are in the flesh. And "the mind that is set on the flesh is hostile to God." Romans 8:7 (ESV). Therefore, "those who are in the flesh cannot please God." Romans 8:8 (ESV). In fact, "without faith it is impossible to please Him." Hebrews 11:6.

That may sound a bit too black-and-white for our "inclusive" culture in America, which has given rise to an "inclusive" message in many congregations. But think about it. Until we're saved, we're citizens of Satan's kingdom. We are slaves to sin, and the wages of sin is death. What glory does God take in that?

But take heart! We know that God takes "no pleasure in

the death of the wicked." Ezek. 33:11. He "desires all people to be saved and to come to knowledge of the truth." 1 Timothy 2:4 (ESV). God patiently endures wicked men, "not wishing that any should perish, but that all should reach repentance." 2 Peter 3:9 (ESV).

Why does He desire that all men reach repentance? That "He might make known the riches of His glory on the vessels of mercy [us whom He called]." Romans 9:23. So, in God's mercy toward us, in saving the otherwise unsaveable, He demonstrates His glory—His infinite, intrinsic value.

Make sure you catch that. God was already glorious, whether He chose to save us or not. In other words, it's not the fact that He chose to save us that makes Him glorious. Salvation merely *demonstrates* His glory, showing His indescribable love in Christ's death for us while we were yet sinners. Romans 5:8.

God also receives glory in His adopted children. In Romans 9, Paul says that God prepared us "beforehand for glory." Romans 9:23. God prepared believers for glory so that He may be glorified in us. We'll look at just a couple of ways God receives glory through believers.

1. God is glorified by the fruit each of us bear as a "new creation" in Christ (2 Cor. 5:17). Jesus said, "I am the vine, you are the branches. He who abides in Me, and I in him, bears much fruit." John 15:5. And when we bear fruit, Jesus says, "My Father is glorified." John 15:8.

2. One way we glorify the Father is through thanksgiving. God loves it when we respond to Him in love. He doesn't take any pleasure in rituals we perform merely out of obligation. This extends even to our sacrifices of stuff. He says, "Do I eat the flesh of bulls or drink the blood of goats?" Psalm 50:13. Hint: The answer is "no." So what does He

want? He says, "Offer to God a sacrifice of thanksgiving, and perform your vows to the Most High." Psalm 50:12.

Why does God value a heartfelt "thank you" over heartless sacrifices like bulls (or money)? Think about it in earthly terms. How many dads spend the year waiting for Father's Day to roll around so they can receive gifts from their children? Dads out there—do you really crave that tie or electric toothbrush? Even if they get you something you want, they're buying it with your money! How much more true of our Father in heaven, who says, "The silver is mine, and the gold is mine"? Haggai 2:8.

Just like us dads, our heavenly Father would rather have a genuine expression of love. For all the pastors reading this—don't get nervous! I'm not saying that believers shouldn't be giving, and giving generously. All I'm saying is that whether we're sacrificing bulls or money, it doesn't mean anything to God if it isn't accompanied by faith. How many times does God lament in the Old Testament that His people offer sacrifices faithlessly? See, for example, Ezekiel 23:37-39; Amos 5:21-27. Here's the heart that God says should accompany those sacrifices: "What does the LORD require of you but to do justly, to love mercy, and to walk humbly with your God?" Micah 6:8.

Let's bring it forward to today. How many churchgoers put money in the offering plate, yet lack faith? What God wants is the thanksgiving that comes only from those with faith, those who "believe that He is, and that He is a rewarder of those who diligently seek Him." Hebrews 11:6. That's the sacrifice He wants—the sacrifice of thanksgiving. Are you so thankful for God that you cheerfully show your thanksgiving by offering Him everything you have, whether it's your song, your money, your time, or your very life? That brings Him glory! He says, "The one who offers thanksgiving as his sacrifice glorifies me." Psalm 50:22 (ESV).

God is also glorified in the God deeds we do. That's not a typo—I really meant "God deeds," not "good deeds." We see unsaved people doing "good" deeds all the time. But does God take glory in these "good" deeds? Let me ask you a question: are those good deeds motivated by a desire to glorify God? Or by a desire to glorify the doer of the deed? That's not a question exclusively for the unbeliever. We Christians need to ask ourselves the same thing.

In Hebrews, the writer describes "repentance from dead works" as one of the elementary principles of Christ. Hebrews 6:1. Do you think he was just talking about things like sexual immorality and covetousness? I don't think so. I think he was talking about the "good" deeds we do for our own glory, to build our own kingdoms.

But once we repent from our good deeds, and start doing God deeds, we begin fulfilling our purpose of glorifying God. Paul says in Ephesians that "we are His workmanship, created in Christ Jesus for good works, which God prepared beforehand that we should walk in them." Ephesians 2:10. We're one body of Christ, but different members, so it's not surprising that each of us have different gifts. We should use those gifts, whether teaching, leading, building, praying, healing, ministering, giving, etc., for the same purpose: "that in all things God may be glorified through Jesus Christ." 1 Peter 4:11.

3.   The Son glories in His bride

The Father adopts every believer as His child. But not only that, He has designated believers (collectively) for marriage to His Son. If you haven't studied Scripture's revelation of the church as the bride of Christ, it can be a hard concept to wrap your mind around. I'm going to give an overview of it here, but don't just take my word for it—study the Word for yourself.

Just as the Father glories in His adopted children, Jesus glories in His bride. To explain how, I'm going to give some background on the Bible's description of the church as the bride, as well as what the Bible says about Jesus' desire for His bride. Then, with that context, we'll look at how the bride brings Christ glory.

The Bible says that Jesus will marry the church. In Ephesians, Paul quotes the description of marriage from Genesis 2:24: "Therefore a man shall leave his father and mother and hold fast to his wife, and the two shall become one flesh.'" Ephesians 5:31. "So what?" you might ask. Well, Paul next says, "This mystery is profound, and I am saying that it refers to Christ and the church." Ephesians 5:32 (ESV).

That's quite a bomb Paul drops. But that's not the only place we see the church described as the bride of Christ. In 2 Corinthians, Paul worries that the Corinthians will be "led astray from [their] sincere and pure devotion to Christ." 2 Corinthians 11:3 (ESV). In fact, he says that he is jealous for the Corinthians with "a divine jealousy" because he "betrothed [them] to one husband, to present [them] as a pure virgin to Christ." 2 Corinthians 11:2 (ESV).

Before we go on, I want to note that Paul was warning the Corinthian church to avoid getting caught up in a vain conversation about the gospel—that is, a conversation that did not result in salvation. Paul worried that the Corinthians would be led astray by a different gospel, or even a different Jesus. 2 Corinthians 11:4. He compared those preaching a different gospel to "the serpent [who] deceived Eve by his cunning." 2 Corinthians 11:3 (ESV). We know the serpent deceived Eve with a partial truth. He still tries the same thing today, hoping that, through deception, he can hook salvation-seekers into a vain conversation that keeps them from ever coming to a saving knowledge of the Truth. Paul wanted us to join the greater conversation, "the *whole* counsel of God." Acts 20:27.

Ok, now back to how Jesus receives glory in His bride. Paul said the church is betrothed to Christ. In 1 Corinthians, Paul said that even now "he who is joined to the Lord is one spirit with Him." 1 Corinthians 6:17. So in this betrothal period, we are one spirit with Christ. But Paul says that a time will come when it is more than that. He says that Jesus will "present her [that is, the church] to Himself a glorious church, not having spot or wrinkle or any such thing." Ephesians 5:27. Then, Paul says that Jesus and the church will become one flesh. Ephesians 5:31-32. What does that mean exactly? Like Paul says, "This mystery is profound." Ephesians 5:32 (ESV). But Revelation says, "Blessed are those who are called to the marriage supper of the Lamb!" Revelation 19:9. For now, let's leave it at this: "There are three things which are too wonderful for me, yes, four which I do not understand: . . . the way of a man with a virgin." Proverbs 30:18-19.

Jesus really wants His bride. In John 17, He says, "Father, I desire that they also whom You gave Me may be with Me where I am, that they may behold My glory which You have given Me." John 17:24. What a powerful statement given that Jesus was only hours from the cross! Knowing what was coming, Jesus presented His supplication to the Father. He desired His bride to be with Him. Amazing! But more than that, Jesus says He wants her to see Him in His glory.

John 17 isn't the only place Jesus expresses that He is glorified by His Bride's attention. For example, many understand the Old Testament's Song of Solomon as more than just a picture of earthly marriage—they understand it to also describe the relationship between Christ and (collectively) believers. Viewed in this light, the Song of Solomon says incredible things about how Jesus glories in His bride. For example, the bridegroom says, "You have ravished my heart, my sister, my spouse, with one look of your eyes." Song of Solomon 4:9. This is how your King feels about you!

That's incredible, but the next line may be even harder to believe. The bridegroom says, "How beautiful is your love, my sister, my bride!" Song of Solomon 4:10 (ESV). If you're like me, you might ask yourself, "How could He say that about *my* love, which is so weak compared to His perfect love?" You might ask, "How could the King of kings, glorified by the Father, possibly care about receiving glory from a bride made up of a bunch of ex-slaves to sin?"

Great questions. The answer: He sees the end from the beginning. In John 17, Jesus says, "the glory which You gave Me, I have given them." John 17:22. What! John earlier testified about seeing this glory that Jesus received from the Father, saying, "we beheld His glory, the glory as of the only begotten of the Father, full of grace and truth." John 1:14. The glory—the infinite, inherent value—that the Father gave Jesus, He gave to us? The Bible says, "Yes!"

John circles back to this point in his first letter, saying, "Beloved, now we are children of God; and it has not yet been revealed what we shall be, but we know that when He [Jesus] is revealed, we shall be like Him, for we shall see Him as He is." 1 John 3:2. What will that look like? When we see Him, we shall see Him in His glory, just as He desires. And then we shall be like Him! What does that mean? Paul tells us in Philippians, saying that "the Lord Jesus Christ . . . will transform our lowly body that it may be conformed to His glorious body." Philippians 3:20-21. This makes sense, because the bridegroom cannot be unequally yoked with the bride. 2 Corinthians 6:14-15.

If you buy into what these verses are saying about Jesus' plan for us believers, you're probably still asking, "Why, Jesus, why?" In the beginning, "the Lord God said, 'It is not good that the man should be alone; I will make him a helper suitable for him." Genesis 2:18 (NASB). Just as Paul understood that Genesis 2's definition of marriage referred to Christ and the church, is it possible that the same is true of this statement?

Going back to that conversation that has been going on throughout eternity, could the Father have said of the Son, the Man on the throne, "It is not good that the Man should be alone"? And then made a helper, a bride, suitable for Him? Not suitable based on her own works, but through an amazing plan of salvation, foreknown before the foundation of the world?

Again, it would sure be easy to get the idea that salvation is all about us. But in 1 Corinthians, Paul says, "Man was not created for the woman's sake, but woman for the man's sake." 1 Corinthians 11:8 (NASB). Indeed! The bride was created for Jesus! But more than that, Paul says that "woman is the glory of man." 1 Corinthians 11:7. In the same way, we've seen that Scripture tells us that the bride is the glory of Christ. Incredible!

When the bride sees Jesus in His glory, she will marvel at Him. 2 Thessalonians 1:10; Revelation 19:7. Having been glorified through Him (Philippians 3:21; 1 John 3:2), she will return that glory to Him. Paul says that in that day Jesus comes, He will "be glorified in His saints and [will] be admired among all those who believe." 2 Thessalonians 1:10. The book of Revelation gives more detail on the response of the redeemed when they appear before Jesus. They will cry "out with a loud voice, saying, 'Salvation belongs to our God who sits on the throne, and to the Lamb.'" Revelation 7:10. Not only that, but the angels will fall on their faces before the throne, worshipping God and saying, "Amen! Blessing and glory and wisdom, thanksgiving and honor and power and might, be to our God forever and ever." Revelation 7:11-12. Truly, the bride will glorify Jesus.

If you have trouble connecting with how the bride brings Jesus glory, think about an earthly wedding ceremony—especially one between two young believers in Jesus.[11] When we go to a wedding, we often say that the bride is radiant. Why? Because, like the Scripture says, she is the glory of her husband. 1 Corinthians 11:7. He commits to loving her like his own flesh, to nourishing her and cherishing her. A bride basks in that glory, and she reflects that glory onto her husband.

A virtuous wife is more precious than rubies. Proverbs 31:10. She brings him praise through her works, as Proverbs 31 describes. But even more than that, she champions him to others. When they ask, "What is your beloved more than another beloved?" she responds by glorifying him so extravagantly that they respond, "Where has your beloved gone . . . that we may seek him with you?" Song of Solomon 5:9-6:1.

And maybe most importantly, she glorifies him when it's just the two of them. She knows his love for her. She says, "I am my beloved's, and his desire is toward me." Song of Solomon 7:10. She longs for time alone with him. She says, "Come, my beloved, let us go forth . . . I will give you my love." Song of Solomon 7:11-12. That love "is as strong as death." Song of Solomon 7:6. Her love is not for sale at any price. She says, "If a man would give for love all the wealth of his house, it would be utterly despised." Song of Solomon 8:7.

Like Paul, I'm telling you this is about Jesus and the

---

[11] We can think of the earthly marriage God designed as a shadow of this heavenly marriage, similar to how Scripture tells us that the earthly tabernacle was a mere shadow of the heavenly tabernacle. Hebrews 8:5.

church. Jesus is the source of His bride's glory. John 17:22. The bride reflects that glory back on to her husband. Revelation 19:7. She will work for Him. She will evangelize for Him. She will praise Him. She will spend time with Him, just the two of them. And her love is for none other than Him. If Satan offers the very kingdoms of the world for her love, she will despise him. That's how the bride glorifies Jesus!

To wrap this section up, remember that the church could not be the bride who glorifies her husband without Jesus' work on the cross. So we can see that the bride's redemption is yet another way the cross is, first and foremost, about God's glory. God gets glory when we receive forgiveness and His salvation. What do we do when we receive them? We praise Him for who He is and what He has done! "I will praise You, for You have answered me." Psalm 118:21. "Oh come, let us sing to the LORD! Let us shout joyfully to the Rock of our salvation!" Psalm 95:1. "Sing to the LORD, bless His name. Proclaim the good news of His salvation from day to day." Psalm 96:2.

If we can just grasp the amazing reality of Jesus' love for His church, how could we fail to pour out our lives as a living sacrifice? How could we be led astray to chase after a different Jesus? What false Jesus could compare to the true Jesus? Lord, empower us through the Holy Spirit to love like You love, to spend our lives glorifying You!

D. The Restoration of All Things in the Age to Come

I spent the most time in convincing you that the cross is about God, His Kingdom, and His Glory since that's the part of the Bible we spend the most time talking about. But I don't want to end this section without talking about where the story goes. Because the cross isn't the end of the story; it's only a new beginning for those who inherit eternal life. The story goes on and on in the age to come. Mark 10:30.

That is some good news within itself. This age is just a chapter of the grander story called eternity. Let me encourage those who are in love with Him and His culture: if life is good now, it only gets better; and if this life is rough now, remember it is short in comparison to eternity. Eternity with Him is not rough at all; it is perfect. With that encouragement, I want to ask, what is the next age all about? It is all about God! His Glory! One Kingdom!

My goal is not to convince you of any particular doctrine about the end times, but to look at the bigger picture that every believer can embrace. Jesus gave John the apostle some information about what's coming in the next age: "Now I saw a new heaven and a new earth, for the first heaven and the first earth had passed away." Revelation 21:1. Not only that, but John "saw the holy city, New Jerusalem, coming down out of heaven from God." Revelation 21:2.

"But wait!" you might ask, "I thought we were going to heaven to be with God forever?" We will be with God forever, but heaven comes to earth! And it's not just the New Jerusalem coming to earth. God comes, too! He won't be a distant Father. And it will be a personal relationship: "Behold, the tabernacle of God is with men, and He will dwell with them, and they shall be His people. God Himself will be with them and be their God." Revelation 21:3. Amen! Did you hear that! We will be with God, and He will be our God! Yay, Jesus! This leaves no doubt that the next age is about God.

The next age is also about God's Glory. In fact, God's Glory shines so brightly in the New Jerusalem that John said, "[t]he city had no need of the sun or of the moon to shine in it, for the glory of God illuminated it." Revelation 21:23. There will be no more darkness because of the presence of God. This is an amazing concept. Proverbs teaches us that "the glory of children is their father" (Prov. 17:6), and in the New Jerusalem, God's children will be there with Him to bask in His glory. My heart lights up thinking that I will be with my Father. We get to bask and soak in our Father's glory!

The next age is also about God's Kingdom. Spoiler alert: Satan is called the god of this age, but he's not the god of the next age. Amen! Satan makes one last stand against God, but it ends up not being much of a battle. Fire comes down from God and devours his army. Revelation 20:7-9. Then he gets cast into the lake of fire (Revelation 20:10), "the eternal fire prepared for the devil and his angels." Matthew 25:41. With that, his rebellion ends, along with mankind's. Christ "puts an end to all rule and all authority and power." 1 Corinthians 15:24. He will "reign till He has put all enemies under His feet"—including death itself. 1 Corinthians 15:26. At that point, He delivers the kingdom to God the Father. 1 Corinthians 15:24.

God will still be God; the reign will be His. The New Jerusalem will include "the throne of God and of the Lamb." Revelation 22:1. The river of the water of life will proceed from the throne of God and of the Lamb. The Tree of Life, from which mankind was barred when Adam and Eve were expelled from the garden, will stand in the city, bearing fruit for those who obeyed His commandments because they loved Him. Revelation 22:2, 14; John 14:15.

This Kingdom of God's will be very good—"there shall be no more curse." Revelation 22:3. But the absence of the curse means that the cause of the curse is also absent. The gates of the New Jerusalem are open only to those who are written in the Lamb's Book of Life, those who abide in His commandments to believe in the name of His Son Jesus Christ and love one another. Revelation 22:14, 21:27; 1 John 3:23. Who is left outside? "Dogs and sorcerers and sexually immoral and murderers and idolaters, and whoever loves and practices a lie." Revelation 22:15.

Focus on those last words—those who don't enter God's eternal Kingdom are those who love and practice a lie. What's the lie? Look at who Paul says will suffer "everlasting destruction from the presence of the Lord and from the glory of His power." 2 Thessalonians 1:9. He says it is those who "do not know God," those who "do not obey the Gospel of our Lord Jesus Christ." 2 Thessalonians 1:8.

God's judgment is not random. Those who suffer everlasting destruction rejected the Good News of Lord Jesus Christ, the Anointed King and His culture. Why? Because they loved and practiced the lie that they could be their own king/god. Those who will not enter are ones who never repented of their treason. In fact, they loved the idea of being their own king even while living in the midst of creation witnessing to them that they were never really a king at all. Romans 1:18-25. In other words, they love the lie. We must take to heart the words of Jesus in the parable of the minas: "Bring here those enemies of mine, who did not want me to reign over them, and slay them before me." Luke 19:27. God would rather the wicked turn from their ways and live (Ezek. 18:23), but God will not have another rebellion against Him and what He loves.

We cannot shy away from this truth. First, we'd be failing to recognize that God is glorified in exercising judgment—

and that He brings judgment to a good end: "The LORD of hosts shall be exalted in judgment, and God who is holy shall be hallowed in righteousness." Isaiah 5:16. With His judgment, He will break the rule of the wicked. This is demonstrated in, for example, Isaiah's prophecy against the king of Babylon: "The Lord has broken the staff of the wicked, the scepter of rulers . . . that ruled the nations in anger with unrelenting persecution." Isaiah 14:6. What was the result of God's judgment on the wicked? "The whole earth is at rest and quiet; they break forth into singing." Isaiah 14:7.

Second, failing to acknowledge God's coming judgment on those who reject His reign and culture does no service to anyone—especially those who are still rejecting His Kingdom. Remember that when He returns, the words "King of kings and Lord of lords" will be written on His thighs and He will establish His throne with judgment for those who rejected His kingdom for their own. He will also fully establish His Kingdom with mercy and grace for those that fell out of love with their own kingdom and learned to love His Kingdom. We must learn to love what God loves and hate what He hates—starting with our desire to be the king of our own lives. When we hate what He hates, we can say along with David, "The fear of the Lord is clean, enduring forever; The judgments of the Lord are true and righteous altogether. More to be desired are they than gold." Psalm 19:9-10. When we love what He loves, then we can say along with the living creatures before the throne in Heaven, "Holy, holy, holy, Lord God Almighty, who was and is and is to come!" Revelations 4:8 (NKJV). Our hearts will be filled with joy and peace—we won't be shaken by anything except the presence of God.

This brings us back around to the importance of understanding the greater conversation—of not being satisfied with a partial conversation. If we only listen to the parts of a conversation that seem to benefit ourselves—for example, "Jesus died for your sins"—we might miss the rest of the conversation, the whole counsel of God, that is "able to make you wise for salvation through faith in Christ Jesus." 2 Tim. 3:15 (ESV). Notice that Paul didn't say, "through faith in *Savior* Jesus." He said in *Christ* Jesus. The Messiah. The Anointed One. The Sovereign. The King.

Jesus said, "Who do you say that I am?" If our answer is not Lord (that is, King), but merely "Savior," I'm afraid that we lived a vain conversation and never understood the greater conversation. We exchanged the truth of God for a lie—that we could have a savior while remaining the king of our own life. We receive salvation when we embrace the revelation of who Jesus is; that is, when we accept His Kingdom—the King and His culture. This is how Luke describes the salvation of the Samaritans in Acts 8: "When they believed Philip as he preached the things concerning the kingdom of God and the name of Jesus Christ, both men and women were baptized." Acts 8:12.

E.   Joining the Greater Conversation

I hope that you agree with me that the main subject of God's conversation—the greater conversation—is not the redemption of man, the forgiveness of our sins, the church, or even the cross. Instead, the subject of the conversation is about God, His Glory, and His one Kingdom!

I'm not downplaying the redemption of man, the forgiveness of our sins, the miracles, the church, and definitely not the work of the cross (we'll talk more about the cross later). But I do want us to understand these topics in the proper context. They are each key elements of the story, but they are key because each plays a part in God getting the glory and establishing His one Kingdom.

It is so important to realize that the conversation is not about us but Him. The Great I AM! The best part of this whole thing is that when we are all about Him, then He can be all about us. But if I make it about me, there is no room for Him to be about me. While we are the object of the conversation, He is the subject.

This is true even when it appears like we are the only one benefiting from God's action. Let's look at an example—Jesus healing the sick. Of course, Jesus cared for the sick people He healed. But His main purpose in doing miracles was the glory of His Father!

If you're not buying it, look at Luke 17. Here, Jesus heals ten lepers. Only one of these lepers came back and glorified God—and the one that did was a Samaritan (who the Jews considered to be repugnant idolaters). Here was Jesus' response: "were there not ten cleansed? But where are the nine? Were there not any found who returned to give glory to God except this foreigner?" Luke 17:17-18. Jesus sees that this one man's response was the purpose of the miracle—to give God the glory.

What about the nine others? I'm sure they were glad to be healed. But did they love God, or did they just love what He could do? I think we see the answer in their response (or lack thereof). Did God get the glory?

In Psalm 79, Israel cries out to the Lord, "Help us, O God of our salvation, for the glory of Your name; and deliver us, and provide atonement for our sins; for Your name's sake!" Psalm 79:9. Hallelujah that He listened to this psalm, that He delivered us for the Glory of His name! And now that He has delivered us, let this be our response: "We, Your people and sheep of Your pasture, will give You thanks forever." Psalm 79:13. We are the sheep of His pasture, the citizens of His Kingdom—let us praise Him forever!

IV.   The Sin and Why a King

We've come a long way. We've searched the Scripture and seen that the Gospel—the Good News—is the King and His culture. We've seen that the whole conversation of the Bible is about God, His Glory, and His Kingdom.

By embracing these Scriptural truths, it becomes so much easier to align ourselves with God's will. Like the psalmist said, "Delight yourself also in the LORD, and He shall give you the desires of your heart." Psalm 37:4. But if we're still stuck in a partial conversation—trying to make the conversation about us instead of Him—we're going to constantly find ourselves out of alignment with God. If we keep making it about us, we become futile in our thinking— "always learning and never able to come to the knowledge of the truth." 2 Timothy 3:7. At worst, this becomes a vain conversation. 1 Peter 1:18.

We avoid living a vain conversation by understanding our position in relationship to God. Imagine that the earth could change the path of its orbit around the sun. If the earth confessed that maintaining its unique life-fostering environment depends on its position with respect to the sun, it would not neglect where it stands with the sun. But what if the earth didn't appreciate that importance? What if the earth even thought that the sun would change its ways to make sure the earth stayed in perfect position?

That might lead the earth to arrogantly approach the sun, discovering the reality that the sun would not bend to the earth's will. What would happen? The Bible actually tells us: "Behold, the day is coming, burning like an oven, and all the proud, yes, all who do wickedly, will be stubble. And the day which is coming shall burn them up." Malachi 4:1.

Such is the importance of our conversation with God. If

we think He exists to please us (even though He loves to), we will never come into alignment with Him, but will instead treat Him with arrogance. But if we grasp that He is the subject of the conversation—"if we fear [His] name," we will be like the earth in perfect alignment with the sun: "The Sun of Righteousness will rise with healing in his wings. And you will go free, leaping with joy like calves let out to pasture." Malachi 4:2 (NLT).

I'd rather be like the calf leaping for joy than the stubble burned in the oven. I hope you feel the same. So, I want to make sure I bring home the key reason that we (mankind) are so susceptible to living a vain conversation with God (that is, believing that God exists to please us, rather than understanding that we exist to bring Him glory). That reason is "the sin."

As we begin exploring the sin, I will (as usual) start with some questions. We already learned that Jesus came preaching, "Repent, for the kingdom of heaven is at hand." Matthew 4:17. What was Jesus telling people to repent (that is, turn away) from? And why was Jesus telling people to repent because the kingdom—the King and His culture—was at hand?

Let's take a journey into the Bible to see what it tells us about *the* sin. We'll find that repentance from the sin is intertwined with Jesus' Kingdom—the two cannot be divorced. If we can grasp this, it will change our paradigm (our worldview) and cause the culture of our hearts to become more like the Father's culture in heaven.

A. The Lamb of God Who Takes Away *the* Sin of the World

As we begin to explore the sin, I want to start by talking about Jesus. Not because He is the sin, of course, but because

He is the antidote to the sin.

The apostle John opens his account of Jesus' life by giving the testimony of a different John, John the Baptist. John the Baptist's public ministry started before Jesus'. He was camped out in the wilderness, wearing camel's hair, eating locusts and honey, when a revival broke out. Matthew 3:1-4.

But this wasn't random—you can't have revival without the Holy Spirit, and the Holy Spirit doesn't act randomly, but according to His will. John's father prophesied through the Holy Spirit that John would "go before the face of the Lord to prepare His ways, to give knowledge of salvation to His people by the remission of their sins, through the tender mercy of our God." Luke 1:76-77. And that's what happened—John did these things, and he did it by preaching the Gospel of the Kingdom.

1. John the Baptist's message: "fire and brimstone" or "love wins!"?

John's mission was to prepare the way for the Lord, giving knowledge of salvation by the remission of sins, through the tender mercy of God. And in just a bit, we're going to see that John identified Jesus as the One who would take away *the* sin of the world. That sounds like good news, right? It is!

But what if you were a Jewish person in Israel waiting for that good news and, when it finally came, it didn't sound like you expected? Maybe it even sounded a little harsh to you. Or even judgmental, to your ears. Would you still think it was good news? Or would you wait for something that sounded more appealing to you? I want to take a look at the message of John the Baptist, forerunner to the King, to make sure we see the good news in it. If we can, we'll be much better prepared to see the good news in the arrival of the King Himself.

At first glance, John's message may not seem effective in drawing people to God. His message was blunt: "Repent, for the kingdom of heaven is at hand!" Matthew 3:1-2. And John didn't avoid preaching about hell either. When the Jewish religious leaders came to check out what was going on, he said to them, "You brood of vipers! Who warned you to flee from the wrath to come? . . . Every tree that does not bear good fruit is cut down and thrown into the fire." Luke 3:7-9 (ESV).

A lot of people consider John to be a "fire and brimstone" preacher based on words like this. But was John's message unduly negative? Or was it the full counsel of God? John said that the Messiah was coming to baptize with the Holy Spirit. Matthew 3:11. That's good news, right? The Jews had been waiting for the Messiah for more than a thousand years. And while John said that the chaff (those who reject God) would be burned with unquenchable fire, John also said that the Messiah would gather His wheat into the barn. Matthew 3:12. We know from the parable of the wheat and the tares that it's a great thing to be God's wheat—it means you're a son of the Kingdom and will shine like the sun! Matthew 13:36-43.

Is it possible that whether we consider John's message to be an "encouraging word" or a "hard word" depends on our perspective? And maybe that perspective can be influenced by the culture around us, which resists the idea that God would ever judge anyone—even those who reject Him? If someone believes that a loving God would never judge anyone, he probably won't like John's message. But if you believe God could righteously judge us all, you will view John's message as good news indeed! And in fact, that's how the Gospel of Luke characterizes John's message: "he preached good news to the people." Luke 3:18.

I'm not sure John would get a job in many churches today. But I guess he didn't have one then either—that's why he was in the wilderness. Yet the people flooded into the wilderness to hear John's message of repentance: "Then Jerusalem, all Judea, and all the region around the Jordan went out to him." And they didn't just hang out in the back row; they "were baptized by him in the Jordan, confessing their sins." Matthew 3:5-6.

Even when John called the Pharisees a brood of vipers, he wasn't being nasty for the sake of it. He was giving the Pharisees an opportunity to own who they were. Remember John's mission: "go before the face of the Lord to prepare His ways, to give knowledge of salvation to his people by the remission of their sins, through the tender mercy of our God." Luke 1:76-77. John knew the Lord was coming, and these guys needed to repent. About three years later, Jesus proved John correct. He likewise called the Pharisees a "brood of vipers." Matthew 23:33. And like John, Jesus asked them a question. But instead of asking who warned them to flee from the coming wrath, Jesus asked, "How are you to escape being sentenced to hell?" Matthew 23:33 (ESV). Hard words, but it got harder when Jesus said that upon them would come "all the righteous blood shed on the earth." Matthew 23:35. Remember that these guys conspired to kill Jesus, the Messiah, just a few days later.

John recognized the precarious state of the Pharisees: that they were whitewashed tombs—shiny and clean on the outside, but full of dead men's bones. Matthew 23:27. John knew that the tender mercies of God were available to these men, but he also knew that they couldn't receive the tender mercies of God unless they themselves recognized their precarious state.

Think about a parable Jesus told another Pharisee. This Pharisee, named Simon, had invited Jesus to eat in his house. After Jesus was seated at the table, a sinful woman came in and anointed His feet with a fragrant oil. She washed His feet with her tears and wiped them with her hair. Luke 7:36-38. Imagine this scene from the Pharisee's perspective. He had invited this teacher into his house (probably thinking he was doing Him a big favor). Now he's got this known sinner in his house, causing a huge commotion with her tears. Not to mention the smell of all that perfume—he was probably thinking, "Who knows how long it'll take for that to clear out!"

Luke says that the "Pharisee spoke to himself . . . if He were a prophet, [He] would know who and what manner of woman this is who is touching Him, for she is a sinner." Luke 7:39. Jesus must have given him a shock when He answered his thoughts, saying, "Simon, I have something to say to you." Luke 7:40.

Jesus then tells a parable about a moneylender who had two guys that owed him money. One owed 500 day's wages, and the other owed 50. Neither could pay the moneylender back, and he freely forgave them both. Jesus concluded with a question: "Tell Me, therefore, which of them will love him more?" Luke 7:41-42.

The Pharisee gives the right answer: "I suppose the one whom he forgave more." Jesus gives him credit for the right answer, but then it gets ugly for Simon. Jesus says, "Do you see this woman? I entered your house; you gave Me no water for My feet, but she has washed My feet with her tears and wiped them with the hair of her head." And then Jesus says, "You gave Me no kiss, but this woman has not ceased to kiss My feet since the time I came in." Jesus finishes it off with the one that probably annoyed Simon the most since it smelled up the house, "You did not anoint My head with oil, but this woman has anointed My feet with fragrant oil." And then Jesus adds the kicker, "Therefore I say to you, her sins, which are many, are forgiven, for she loved much. But to whom little is forgiven, the same loves little."

Luke 7:43-47.

Now think back to John and the brood of vipers. If they didn't recognize that they were a brood of vipers, Jesus said that all the righteous blood shed on earth would come on their heads. But if they recognized who they were, like the sinful woman recognized her sin, the tender mercies of God were right there waiting for them. They would be forgiven much, and they would love much. And love would win!

We know that some of them did reach this understanding. Nicodemus, a Pharisee, helped Joseph of Arimathea prepare Jesus' body for burial. And the book of Acts refers to "some of the sect of the Pharisees who believed." Acts 15:5. So even the brood of vipers can flee from the coming wrath—if they recognize the danger. With that in mind, let me ask, was John's message of warning to the Pharisees a "fire and brimstone" message or a message of love? If we can recognize the love in John's message, we're on the right track toward viewing the Bible from God's perspective, rather than man's, and receiving the One who takes away *the* sin of the world.

2.   "Repent, for the kingdom of heaven is at hand"

Let's zoom in on John's catch phrase—"Repent, for the kingdom of heaven is at hand." The Kingdom was at hand, meaning the King was near. When people started wondering if John himself was the Christ (the King) they were waiting for, he told them he was not. Another was coming: "I indeed baptize you with water; but One mightier than I is coming, whose sandal strap I am not worthy to loose." Luke 3:15-16. But John didn't just know who he wasn't; he knew who he was. John knew his identity, saying, "I am the voice of one crying in the wilderness: Make straight the way of the LORD." John 1:23. Don't miss this—whose way was John making straight? The Lord. That's actually "LORD" in all caps because he's specifically referring to Yahweh, the name God used for Himself in the Old Testament. John was saying that he was preparing the way for Yahweh God.

The very next day, John saw that One, the One mightier than him, the One whose paths he was making straight—Yahweh God become flesh. When John sees Jesus coming toward him to be baptized, John makes a powerful proclamation: "Behold! The Lamb of God who takes away the sin of the world!" John 1:29.

We have to look carefully to catch the full depth of this foundational verse. Why does John say that the Lamb takes away "*the* sin" of the world? Did Jesus take away only one sin? If so, I hope it's mine! But even that wouldn't do me much good, because I created such a long record of sin! Seriously, though, we know Jesus took away all sins. In fact, John (the apostle) himself says in 1 John that "the blood of Jesus Christ cleanses us from all sin." 1 John 1:7.

Since Jesus cleanses us from all sin, why does John say Jesus takes away "the sin"? Let's talk about the "the." In the chapter "What is the gospel?" I explained that "the" is a definite article. A definite article refers to a specific thing, something the author expects the audience to be familiar with. In contrast, an indefinite article like "a" doesn't refer to a particular thing. For example, we say "the church" when talking about the body of Christ as a whole. We say "a church" when talking generally about a local church.

In John 1:29, John refers to "the sin." Singular, not plural. And John didn't say "a sin," he said "the sin." That means he's talking about a specific sin, a sin that he expects the audience to be familiar with. This is "*the* sin" that Jesus came to take away. The main sin, or the root of all sins.

B.   What is *the* sin?

1.   Young's Literal Translation

John 1:29 is not the only verse in the New Testament where the phrase "the sin" is used in the original Greek language in which the New Testament was written. However, most English translations don't translate this phrase as "the sin," outside of this particular verse. Instead, they generally translate it as simply "sin." We're going to look at some of those verses, but to get as close as possible to a word-for-word translation of the original Greek, we're going to use Young's Literal Translation (YLT) of the Bible.

Different Bible versions approach translating the Scripture in different ways, varying in how literally they translate the original language. For example, the New King James Version (NKJV), the English Standard Version (ESV), and the New American Standard Bible (NASB) generally attempt to translate the Greek into English word-for-word. But they sometimes deviate from that general principle in a good-faith effort to render an accurate translation, since two different languages don't always match up well on a word-for-word basis. This translation style is referred to as formal equivalence. Other translations, like the New Living Translation (NLT), will translate a phrase more loosely if, in the translator's opinion, that will be easier for the reader to understand. This translation style is called dynamic equivalence. While a dynamic-equivalence translation like the NLT can be a helpful resource, formal-equivalence translations are generally better for serious Biblical study.

Back to Young's Literal Translation. The YLT was made by Robert Young and first published in 1862. As the name says, the YLT endeavors to provide a strictly literal translation of the original Hebrew and Greek texts. While that (along with the fact that it was translated 150 years ago) sometimes makes the English translation read less smoothly than other translations, its strictly literal style makes it ideal for our purposes in this chapter.

2. Identifying the sin from God's perspective

In seeking to identify *the* sin that Jesus took away, we're going to jump forward in John to chapter 8, where he quotes Jesus talking about the sin. In verse 34, Jesus says, "Verily, verily, I say to you—Every one who is committing sin, is a servant of *the* sin." John 8:34 (YLT). When we sin, we are a servant to "the sin!" The sin enslaves us and we obey it.

But that still leaves us wondering—what is "the sin"? In particular, what is "the sin of the world" that the Lamb of God takes away? Let's go back to the greater conversation and look again at the first sin ever recorded. I believe it will help shed light on what "the sin" is. Recall that the conversation has been, is, and always will be about God, His glory, and His kingdom. That was certainly true before the beginning, before God had created heavenly or earthly beings. And it was true for some period of time thereafter. But then Lucifer rebelled, preferring to rule a domain of darkness rather than serve in God's Kingdom. He became the god of this age, the ruler of this world, the prince of the power of the air. What did Lucifer do that got him kicked out of the presence of God?

Let's look again at Isaiah's prophetic picture of Lucifer's fall: "How you are fallen from heaven, O Lucifer, son of the morning!" Isaiah 14:12. "For you have said in your heart: I will ascend into heaven, I will exalt my throne above the stars of God; I will also sit on the mount of the congregation on the farthest sides of the north; I will ascend above the heights of the clouds." And then the kicker: "I will be like the Most High." Isaiah 14:13-14.

Lucifer was kicked out of heaven for his desire. Five times, Lucifer says, "I will." He wanted *his* will! What was his will? Ultimately, he wanted to "be like the Most High." He wanted the throne of God. He wanted to be glorified. He wanted to be his own lord, king, and great I AM. He wanted to be the Most *High*, which explains why the other four desires were all about being lifted up: (1) *ascend* into heaven; (2) exalt my throne *above* the stars of God; (3) sit *on* the mount of the congregation; and (4) ascend *above* the heights of the clouds. Isaiah 14:13-14. He wanted to be the highest of the High, to take a throne and be the king.

The first sin—which is the root of all sins—is the desire to be the king, the one who sits on the throne, *the* sin.

3.   The sin seduces mankind

We next see the sin (the desire to be king) at work in the garden of Eden. We find Eve engaging in a conversation with the serpent, who was Satan, the firstborn of the sin. Satan presents his favorite question, which he has since asked countless times of countless people over the years: "Did God actually say . . .?" In posing this question to Eve, he asked, "Did God actually say, 'you shall not eat of any tree in the garden?'" Genesis 3:1 (ESV).

In questioning God's command not to eat of the Tree of Knowledge of Good and Evil, Satan starts by trying to spur doubt in Eve's heart about the word of God. He wanted Eve to doubt God so he could then take it a step further. Satan rarely asks us to deny God with his first question. He's the subtlest of all creatures, and he leads us to do so in small steps that, individually, don't seem like a big deal.

Eve replies by disagreeing with Satan, saying they could "eat of the fruit of the trees in the garden, but God said, 'You shall not eat of the fruit of the tree that is in the midst of the garden, neither shall you touch it, lest you die.'" Genesis 3:2-3. We can see her first mistake before we even get into what she said. The first mistake was saying anything all. She should not have engaged in conversation with the enemy. Instead, she should have submitted to God, resisted the devil, and he would have fled from her. James 4:17. But we do the same thing all the time. Why? Because he's the subtlest of all creatures, and we don't recognize his attacks for what they are.

The serpent then replies that "she will not die." He contradicts the direct statement of God. He proceeds to say that, if she eats of the tree, she will be like God. Read Satan's reply: "You will not surely die. For God knows that when you eat of it your eyes will be opened, and you will be like God, knowing good and evil." Genesis 3:4-5 (ESV). He tempts her with the power of being like God. The same desire that led to his fall, he used to tempt Eve.

She took the bait. Eve "saw that the tree was good for food, and that it was a delight to the eyes, and that the tree was to be desired to make one wise, [and] she took of its fruit and ate." Genesis 3:6 (ESV). Satan provided the idea of becoming like God. Eve provided the desire. Satan can't create the desires in us, but he can and does exploit them.

C.   The Desire to be King

James, the brother of Jesus, writes to believers, warning
them against the danger of giving in to their desires: "each
one is tempted, by his own desires being led away and
enticed, afterward the desire having conceived, doth give
birth to sin, and the sin having been perfected, doth bring
forth death." James 1:14-15 (YLT). James tells us that desire
for anything outside of God's commands will lead one
away—but away from what? From God. That's what
happened to Eve, and James warns us not to follow the same
path.

The Greek word for "lead away" can also be translated as
"drag." In other words, when desire is conceived—that is,
when a person submits to a desire contrary to God's
(therefore acting as his own king instead of serving God as
King), the desire will begin to drag him. He may know he
shouldn't go, but he is being dragged. It's important to realize
that our old nature is addicted to our kingdom. Think about
the instructions that recovering addicts receive: they are told
to stay away from anything that might trigger their desire for
that addiction. If they give into their addictive desire, that
desire begins to drag them back until they are once again fully
engaged in their addiction.

James writes his letter to the church. He is writing to those
who have been set free from the addiction to their own
kingdom. He is warning us to not give into the idea of going
back to our own kingdom. I know that when I sin, I need
only confess it and God is faithful and just to cleanse me by
the blood of Christ. 1 John 1:7-9. What makes me uneasy—
and what I asked the Lord for help overcoming—is the desire
that drew me into sin. Receiving forgiveness for a sin does
not mean that my desire to seek my own kingdom
automatically ceases. While the desire for my kingdom will
usually be tamed when the guilty feeling is fresh, given time

and opportunity, that desire will again rise. That desire needs to be addressed as much as a sin needs to be covered by the blood. If I am not sober-minded, preparing for the desire for my kingdom to raise its ugly head, it will drag me back to the place of sin. That is why I must not only repent of my sins, but must begin taking every thought captive, set my mind on His kingdom, and spend time delighting in God, knowing that He will fulfill my desires. 2 Corinthians 10:5; Colossians 3:2; Psalm 37:4.

We know that even though Eve was in perfect relationship with God, she was dragged away from that relationship by her desire to be her own god/queen. If that desire dragged away her who had never known sin (or known what it was like to be her own queen), how much more can it drag away us who have tasted of our own kingdom? Jesus tells us the answer. If someone isn't a believer, Jesus says he is owned by his desire—he is a slave to sin: "Verily, verily, I say to you— Every one who is committing sin, is a servant of the sin." John 8:34 (YLT). There is hope for the unbeliever—that hope lies in becoming poor in spirit. But until he decides he is not king, he will continue to try to be king.

If someone is a born-again believer, the Holy Spirit dwells in him and has set him "free from the law of the sin and of the death" (Romans 8:2 (YLT)), breaking the chains of desire. That's not to say that the believer will never be tempted; rather, the believer now has a choice, the power to resist the desire dragging him toward the sin. And we can trust that our faithful God "will not allow [us] to be tempted beyond what [we] are able, but with the temptation will also make the way of escape, that [we] may be able to bear it." 1 Corinthians 10:13. We might need to resist to the point we have sweat and blood coming out of our pores like Jesus, but He will not take us past what we can bear. This means that we have freedom from *the* sin through Christ, and therefore can't use our desire as an excuse for sinning. God provides the means to escape it.

But when we don't take that route of escape from our kingdom desires, and instead submit to those desires, we are choosing to distrust God, leading us into sin: "the sin having been perfected, doth bring forth death." James 1:15 (YLT). Those who have surrendered their kingdom to God, but later give in to the desire for their own kingdom, find themselves climbing back on to the throne they previously surrendered. In their minds, they're not trying to take the whole throne, just a small area. But once someone starts down that path, the desire drags them to the point where they seize the whole throne of their heart. And then they are again enslaved to their own kingdom, *the* sin.

We can surely agree we don't desire death, so it becomes important to understand what James means when he talks about "the sin" being "perfected." Consider that other translations render this as "maturity" or "fully grown." So how does the root sin—the desire to be king—become fully grown? It starts off as an idea—"wouldn't it be great to be the king?" Or, "Wouldn't it be nice to have my way and my will done now!" When we act on that desire, it gives birth to sin. It may begin as small acts of rebellion ("I know I'm not supposed to look at porn, but it's not really hurting anyone"). And then the sin matures, producing full-blown rebellion: you, God, are not my King. I am my own king. One may not say those words, but their actions/fruit say it. Actually, they may even declare with their lips that God is Lord, but their addiction to their own kingdom shows otherwise. What's the result when *the* sin, the desire to be king, becomes fully grown? Death.

We can see the pattern that James describes at work in Eve's decision to disobey God. Eve desired to be like God; she wanted her way instead of His way. She gave into that desire to be like God, allowing her desire to provoke her to eat the fruit. Her sinful disobedience to God's command was the fruit of the sin—the desire to be her own god, queen, lord, and great I AM. She didn't enter into rebellion because she wanted to know the difference between good and evil; she rebelled against God because she wanted to be god.

We see another example of this process in the Old Testament, during the life of King David. David had a son named Absalom. Absalom desired to be king. Absalom started to rebel against David when another of David's sons, Amnon (Absalom's half-brother), raped Tamar, Absalom's full sister.

While the Bible says that when King David heard of the rape, "he was very angry," the Bible does not report whether he punished Amnon. Regardless, Absalom was clearly not satisfied with the outcome. His anger may have been righteous, but the Bible commands us not to let even righteous anger provoke us to sin: "Be angry, and do not sin." Ephesians 4:26. Absalom's anger was righteous and just in his own eyes and the desire to fulfill his righteousness, his justice, led him to sin.

Two full years after the rape, Absalom persuaded David to get all his sons, including Amnon, to accompany Absalom out of town to a party. But it wasn't much of a party for Amnon, as Absalom had conspired with his servants to murder Amnon once he was drunk on wine. 2 Samuel 13:23-29. He had been planning it from the day Amnon raped Tamar two years earlier. 2 Samuel 13:32.

Absalom sinned in murdering Amnon, but he also sinned by usurping King David's authority. Whether David acted righteously or not, he apparently desired to show leniency to Amnon, and it was not Absalom's place to exact vengeance. While this episode was only the beginning, we can see a desire in Absalom to exercise David's authority—to be the king.

Absalom's desire manifested itself in sin. He was not satisfied with David's handling of the situation, so he took matters into his own hands.

Absalom's desire to be king continued to grow, to mature. He fled the country for a few years after murdering Amnon, until King David eventually allowed him to return. But Absalom's rebellion against the king continued. He began to curry the favor of the people, suggesting to them that King David was withholding justice from them—justice Absalom would give if only he had the opportunity. 2 Samuel 15:1-5. The people bought it: "Absalom stole the hearts of the men of Israel." 2 Samuel 15:6.

Eventually, Absalom's desire to be king became full grown. Once he gathered enough supporters, he declared himself king, saying "Absalom reigns in Hebron!" 2 Samuel 15:9. Like with Satan's treason, Absalom's declaration started a war—his men against King David's men. Twenty thousand men died in a single day, including Absalom. Since "pride goes before destruction" (Proverbs 16:18), I don't think it's a coincidence that Absalom died when his luxuriant hair (which Scripture suggests was a source of pride for him) got caught in a tree as his mule galloped underneath, allowing David's men to catch him and kill him. 2 Sam. 14:25-26; 2 Samuel 15:9-14. The sin, Absalom's desire to be king, became full grown, resulting in his death.

Let me give a note on the King's heart toward those that commit treason. David's reaction to Absalom's death is interesting. After a messenger told David that his men had triumphed over Absalom's, David asked about his son. The messenger replied, "May the enemies of my lord the king and all who rise up against you for evil be like that young man." 2 Samuel 18:32 (ESV). In other words, "He's dead, and I hope all your enemies suffer the same fate." That's a very human reaction. But David didn't think like a king whose enemy suffered the fate he deserved. David thought like a father who lost a son. Even though Absalom committed treason and started a full-scale rebellion, David mourned Absalom greatly.

Remember that David was a man after God's own heart. Acts 13:22. Everyone has committed treason against God, and if they don't repent, they will suffer the same fate as Absalom. But we who have been given victory in Christ should not rejoice like David's messenger. Because God doesn't rejoice. He says, "I have no pleasure in the death of the wicked, but that the wicked turn from his way and live." Ezekiel 33:11. He cries out: "Turn, turn from your evil ways! For why should you die?" Ezekiel 33:11. Paul carries this through to the New Testament, saying that God "desires all men to be saved and to come to the knowledge of the truth." 1 Timothy 2:4. And when one of those men does repent, "there is joy before the angels of God." Luke 15:10.

1.   The sin produces death

Just like James said, when Eve's desire to be god (the sin) became fully grown, it brought forth death. James 1:15. After Eve ate the fruit (followed quickly by Adam), God said, "Behold the man has become like one of Us, to know good and evil." Genesis 3:22. This is a powerful statement by God—He just declared that man had become like Him, at least in knowing good and evil. This led God to drive Adam and Eve out of the garden—lest they "take also of the tree of life, and eat, and live forever." Genesis 3:22.

Why did God want to prevent man from living forever in his sinful state? When God created man, He gave them "dominion . . . over every living thing that moves on the earth" and told them to "fill the earth and subdue it." Genesis 1:28. So man was supposed to control the earth under the paradigm of enjoying God's Lordship. But, after Adam and

Eve sinned by fulfilling their desire to be their own god, they were at enmity with God, no longer submitting to His rule, but doing what was right in their own eyes. They were their own kings. Thus, God sent man out of the garden so they could not eat from the Tree of Life, which would have allowed them to live forever—even in their state of enmity against God.

What would have occurred if men had become immortal while in slavery to sin? The Bible gives us a glimpse of how bad things quickly became even with mortal men. A little more than 1,500 years after Adam's sin, "the Lord saw that the wickedness of man was great in the earth, and that every intent of the thoughts of his heart was only evil continually . . . the earth was filled with violence." Genesis 6:5-6, 11. Sometimes, the fear of death can influence a man's behavior, providing a restraining effect. But what if the man has no fear of death? More than that, what if he knew he was immortal? It's difficult to imagine the chaos that would have resulted if God had allowed man to eat the fruit of the Tree of Life in his sinful state.

In His infinite wisdom and righteousness, God did not allow sinful man to eat of the Tree of Life. Instead, death entered the world through Adam's sin. Romans 5:12. Thus, while God's intention was life, the fruit of man's actions became, and today remains, death. Look at how Paul puts it in 1 Corinthians: "Where, O Death, thy sting? Where, O Hades, thy victory?' And the sting of the death is the sin." 1 Corinthians 15:55-56. Paul identifies "the sin" as the sting of "the death."

2.   God's law reveals our futile desire to be king

Paul doesn't stop at identifying the sin as the sting of death; he goes on to say that "the power of the sin [is] the law." 1 Corinthians 15:56. What did he mean by that? After the Israelites heard the law that God revealed to Moses, the people of Israel "answered with one voice and said, 'All the words which the LORD has said we will do.'" Exodus 24:3. From that point on, the Israelites were not free to do what they thought right; they had to do what they were told.

The Israelites may have agreed to follow the law with the best of intentions, but as Paul explains in Romans, the law gave the sin in them the opportunity to rear its ugly head and produce death in those who would be their own kings: "the sin, having received an opportunity, through the command, did deceive, and through it did slay me." Romans 7:8 (YLT). So the power of "the sin" was revealed in Israel when God gave them the law.

Does that mean that "the law is sin"? Romans 7:7. No! For "through the law comes knowledge of sin." Romans 3:20. Specifically, Paul says that knowledge of sin comes through the law: "but the sin I did not know except through the law." Romans 7:7 (YLT). Applying this to the root sin, unless the King exercises His authority by giving the law, we won't recognize our desire to be our own king. The opportunity for conflict between His kingdom and our kingdom wouldn't arise. And without the knowledge of sinfulness, and ultimately knowledge of *the* sin, what will drive us to repentance? This question becomes critical, as the failure to recognize the sin in us leads to disaster: "A people without understanding shall come to ruin." Hosea 4:14 (ESV).

We can see that the Israelites' desire to be their own god/king caused them to rebel in both heart and body against God's directives. The law proved to them how far they were from God being their King—from loving what He loves and hating what He hates. It revealed that their heart's desire, at its root, was to have their own will and be their own king.

Jesus said that everyone begins with this same heart

problem when He said, "Every one who is committing sin, is a servant of the sin." John 8:34 (YLT). Praise God that the good news also applies to all who believe, Jew and Gentile alike! Like Paul said, "Thanks be to God, who gives us the victory through our Lord Jesus Christ." 1 Corinthians 15:57.

D.   The Sin is Lawlessness

We've now learned that the sin—the desire for man to be his own king—produces rebellion. But why is that? Because the sin is itself rebellion—it is the rejection of God's reign in our life. In fact, the apostle John said the sin is lawlessness: "Every one who is doing the sin, the lawlessness also he doth, and the sin is the lawlessness." 1 John 3:4 (YLT).

The lawless person recognizes no law, leading him to question God's authority (and word). In Romans 9, Paul asks, "O man, who are you to reply against God? Will the thing formed say to him who formed it, 'Why have you made me like this?' Does not the potter have power over the clay?" Romans 9:21. We—mankind formed from the dust of the ground—have no right to question the power of our Creator, yet the lawless person does exactly that. The lawless man does whatever feels right in his eyes, regardless of whether it is right in the eyes of the One who created him. The lawless man has a moral compass that always points in the direction of personal pleasure.

Now, it would be easy to limit the lawless person to those who completely reject God by never noticing Him. But it's more than that. Those who want to use Jesus to further their own kingdom are also lawless. This type of lawless person notices Jesus, but only for what Jesus can do for him. Not for Jesus' intrinsic value. Even the disciples fell into this trap, arguing about who among them would be greatest. Mark 9:34. James and John actually approached Jesus privately to ask for the privilege of sitting on Jesus' right and left when He came into His glory. Mark 10:37. They were following Jesus, but (at this time) were focused on their own position and glory.

Here's an example of how easy it is to allow our inclination toward personal comfort and instant gratification skew our walk with Jesus. In Matthew 16, Peter has an incredible moment. Jesus asks him, "Who do you say that I am?" Matthew 16:15. After Peter answers, "You are the Christ, the Son of the living God" (v. 16), Jesus says that Peter received this revelation (on which His church will be built) from the Father. Not only that, but Jesus tells Peter that He will give him the keys to the Kingdom of Heaven. Matthew 16:19. Pretty awesome, to put it mildly.

You might think that Peter would ride this moment of revelation into a long stretch of wisdom and truth. But that didn't turn out to be the case. The next passage in Matthew 16 says that Jesus began teaching the disciples that He must suffer many things, be killed, and be raised on the third day. Matthew 16:21. Did Peter respond by saying, "I mourn that our sin of treason means this is the only way You can redeem us, but praise God for the obedience of His Son!" Not exactly. He rebuked Jesus, saying, "Far be it from You, Lord; this shall not happen to You!" Matthew 18:22. Jesus' response: "Get behind Me, Satan! You are an offense to Me." Matthew 18:23.

What was Peter's error? Jesus explained: "You are not mindful of the things of God, but the things of men." Matthew 18:23. When we think like men, the desire for personal pleasure and positions draws us away from God. Peter was thinking like a man, and it (temporarily) blinded him to the plan of salvation. Peter, like the rest of the disciples, were following Jesus because they hoped He would deliver them from the Roman Empire, which had enslaved Israel. They believed that He came to set them free from a foreign king and that Jesus the King would sit on the throne in Jerusalem. They understood that they would not have *the* throne, but a throne next to Him. That is why they were wondering who would be the closest to Him. They were interested in what the Kingdom's pecking order would look like.

Peter was a man of his word and was willing to die for such a position. He was the one disciple who pulled out a sword and struck one of the men who came to arrest Jesus. He was willing to die for a position, but (at that time) not for Jesus or His ways. After Jesus' arrest, Peter denied Jesus three times before the rooster crowed twice. Mark 14:72. Peter was interested in Jesus for his own hopes and purposes, not for Jesus' hopes and Kingdom. Peter's hopes included Jesus, but only as Jesus served Peter's agenda. Peter was making choices with his own kingdom, not Jesus' Kingdom, in mind—even though he was in the very presence of Jesus! That is why Jesus tells Peter to get behind Him. Peter was reasoning like a man, which led to Jesus calling him Satan. Peter thought he was giving Jesus wise counsel, but his human reasoning served Satan rather than God. It would lead to death, not life.

1.   Pleasure drives the lawless person

When we try to be our own king, we'll usually let our love for pleasure drive our desires. This makes sense. The king does what he wants, and the king wants pleasure. We see this in the world around us, revealing itself in addiction to pornography, sex, illegal drugs, painkillers, alcohol, power, attention, etc. Paul warned us that it's only going to get worse: "But know this, that in the last days perilous times will come: For men will be lovers of themselves, lovers of money . . . lovers of pleasure rather than lovers of God." 2 Timothy 3:1-4.

When someone allows the desire for pleasure to rule his life, he will cause pain, sorrow, and even death. We looked at a good example of this earlier in this chapter—the story of King David's son Amnon raping his half-sister Tamar. Amnon allowed his desire for pleasure to rule him. He pretended to be sick and asked David to send Tamar to make him some food. In reality, he was lying in wait and, when she wouldn't willingly lie with him, he raped her. 2 Samuel 13:4-

14.

Amnon's act led to pain, suffering, and death. Pain for Tamar, who was raped. And also suffering. After Amnon raped Tamar, he hated the beautiful girl with whom he had been obsessed only moments before. So much so that he actually made his servant kick her out and bolt the door behind her. 2 Samuel 13:15-18. Tamar put ashes on her head and tore the robe of many colors worn by the king's virgin daughters. She mourned bitterly and remained desolate in her brother Absalom's house. 2 Samuel 13:18-20. And, as we read above, Amnon's desire for pleasure ultimately led to his death at the hands of his brother Absalom.

Amnon's story is not an anomaly. While it's ok to like pleasure, the desire for pleasure cannot come close to the desire for God. The one who allows the desire for pleasure to rule his life will cause pain, suffering, and death. It's not a matter of *if*, it's a matter of *when*. That's because, like Paul said, men will be "lovers of pleasure rather than lovers of God." 2 Timothy 3:4. You can't be both. Just like you can't serve both God and money. Matthew 6:24. So if you love pleasure, you won't love God. And if you don't love God, you sure won't love your neighbor like yourself.

Don't be confused—I don't mean that loving God (accepting Him as our King) won't bring pleasure. It will. The Lord is the creator of pleasure and desires us to have pleasure. But we must trust Him to give it to us. King David trusted Him, praising God for giving "drink from the river of Your pleasure." Psalm 36:8. How do we drink from God's river of pleasure? David tells us in the very next psalm: "Delight yourself in the LORD, and He will give you the desires of your heart." Psalm 37:4 (NASB).

We need to delight (take pleasure) in Him, for He has a river of pleasure that flows non-stop. But you must be looking for Him, not your own pleasure. When we make His pleasure our pleasure, He will give us the desires of our hearts.

2. The form of godliness without the heart of godliness

We saw above that Paul warned about the coming days when people would be lovers of pleasure rather than lovers of God. 2 Timothy 3:1-4. Understand that he wasn't talking about heathens. Unbelievers have been lovers of pleasure rather than lovers of God for millennia—nobody needs to wait till the last days to see that. Paul was talking about people who claim to know Jesus. He said these people "have a form of godliness but deny its power." 2 Timothy 3:5.

These folks will be talking the talk and, at least publicly, walking the walk. They might show up for church. They might put their 10% in the offering plate. They might even be leading Bible studies. And some of these lawless people— people who are directed by their compass of pleasure—will actually do miracles.

This last one can be a difficult concept for us to wrap our head around. How can someone operate in the power of the Holy Spirit, yet still desire in his heart to possess his own kingdom? Yet it's true. Look at these words of Jesus: "Not everyone who says to Me, 'Lord, Lord,' shall enter the kingdom of heaven, but he who does the will of My Father in heaven." Matthew 7:21. "Ok, no big deal," you might say. "Of course, you have to do the will of the Father to enter the kingdom." But look at what Jesus says next: "Many will say to Me in that day, 'Lord, Lord, have we not prophesied in Your name, cast out demons in Your name, and done many wonders in Your name?' And then I will declare to them, 'I never knew you; depart from Me, you who practice lawlessness!'" Matthew 7:22-23.

These are truly shocking words! Jesus is saying that many people who do many wonders—people who cast out demons and prophesy—will not enter the Kingdom of Heaven. You might ask, "How could an unsaved person do wonders in the name of Jesus?" A great question, yet we see that the Holy Spirit can and does use unsaved people to do His will.

The apostle John tells us that Caiaphas, who was high priest of the Jews when Jesus was crucified, accurately prophesied "that Jesus would die for the nation, and not for that nation only, but also that He would gather together in one the children of God who were scattered abroad." John 11:49-52. Yet this is the same Caiaphas who shortly thereafter accused Jesus of blasphemy and incited the Jewish leaders to condemn Him to death. Matthew 26:62-65. Hardly someone we would expect the Holy Spirit to move through.

Another example is Balaam, a gentile seer who Balak, the king of Moab, tried to pay to curse Israel as they moved toward the Promised Land. Balaam would have happily done so, except that the Spirit of God came upon him, leaving him unable to do anything but bless Israel. God even used him to prophesy about the Messiah, saying, "A Scepter shall rise out of Israel . . . Out of Jacob One shall have dominion." Numbers 24:9, 17-19. Yet this same seer then told Balak to use Moabite women to seduce the Israelites into sexual immorality and idol worship. Again, not the guy we would expect the Holy Spirit to work through. Numbers 31:16; Numbers 25:1-3; Revelation 2:14.

These examples confirm that a person isn't necessarily a follower of Jesus merely because the Holy Spirit uses him to accomplish God's will. Paul even rejoiced when people preached the (true) Gospel out of selfish ambition. Philippians 1:15-18. He wasn't rejoicing over their selfish ambition, but that the true Gospel was being preached. He could rejoice in this because the power is in the Gospel, not the people who preach it.

So we see that people who look and sound "Christian" aren't necessarily Christ's. Just because their public words and deeds look similar to God's ways does not mean they want God. Many have a desire for God, yet still have an appetite for the sin, wanting to be their own king and wanting God's help in furthering their kingdom. They're doing Christian things, but in their hearts, they're not doing it for God; they're doing it for themselves. In their hearts, they're not subjecting themselves to God's laws; they are lawless. They have the appearance of godliness but deny its power.

E.   The wheat and the tares

Jesus told a parable about wheat and tares that illustrates the folly of being satisfied with the appearance of godliness without ever obtaining a heart of godliness. In this parable, the good farmer (Jesus) goes into His field (the world) and plants good wheat seed (the sons of the kingdom; that is, His children). Later, the farmer's servants come to Him with news that a type of weed, called tares, has sprung up among the wheat. The farmer knows the tares are the work of an enemy—the devil. The farmer's servants offer to pull up the tares. He tells them they have the right idea, but the wrong timing. He tells them to wait until the harvest (the end of the age). At that point, the servants will gather the tares (those of "the sin"), bind them up, and cast them into the furnace of fire, while the wheat will be gathered into the barn (His kingdom). Matthew 13:24-30, 36-43.

1.   For a while, the tares do a good job acting like wheat

As they are growing in the field, the wheat and the tares look alike in the midst of the field (that is, the world). The children of God aren't of the world, but we are in the world. And so are our church buildings, house churches, and every gathering of the brethren. They attract worldly people who believe they are believers, but who walk according to their own sinful desires. Jude 1:16, 19 (ESV). They sometimes gain influence in the church, "flattering people to gain advantage." Jude 1:16. But they are "devoid of the Spirit." Jude 1:19 (ESV). They are not sons of the kingdom; they are blemishes in our churches. Jude 1:12 (NIV). They are tares among the wheat.

But like the parable says, it's hard to tell the difference at first. Both groups of people worship God (or appear to, anyway), say amen, read their Bibles, go to prayer meetings, attend church, do missions, pay tithes, lead, pastor, etc. One group does it because they love God for who He is, and the other loves all that God possesses. The tares want His signs and wonders, while the wheat want Him who *is* the great Wonder and moves in signs and wonders. The tares love the abilities of God for their gain, while the wheat love Him, and see His abilities as an amazing invitation to fall more in love with Him. While the two groups initially look similar, the difference will eventually be revealed. As Paul said, while "some men's sins are clearly evident . . . those of some men follow later." 1 Timothy 5:24.

By the time harvest time rolls around, the wheat and tares become very distinct from one another. Wheat grows what farmers call "a head." As you probably guessed, the head grows at the top of the plant, and it's the part that actually contains the grain (the stuff you make bread out of). As the head grows, the plant becomes top-heavy, causing the stalk to bend. But a tare is just a weed, not a useful plant, and grows no head to harvest. It lacks the fruit of the wheat; therefore, it continues to stand up straight. Did you catch that? Wheat bows and tares stand up straight.

Jesus says, "You will know them by their fruits." Matthew 7:16. Remember that one bows before a king, while one stands before a president. Why the difference? Because people serve a king, whereas a president serves the people. The fruit of the wheat leads them to bow before the King. The fruitlessness of the tares leads them to remain standing before the King because they wrongly think the King is for them. The wheat is about the King, while the tare is about itself.

2.   **Praise be to God that He didn't let the servants pull up the tares right away!**

You might still be asking why the good farmer allows the

tares—the lawless and those who cause sin—to grow in His field along with His wheat (His children)? This can be hard to understand. Jesus says the tares include the lawless and those who cause sin. And they do exactly that, wreaking havoc among the wheat in the world. So why doesn't Jesus allow the servants to destroy the tares right away?

Jesus gave us the answer in the parable itself. When the servants ask to gather the tares immediately, the farmer says, "No, lest while you gather up the tares you also uproot the wheat with them." Matthew 13:29. Think a little more carefully about those tares the servants would be pulling up: all who were lawless and caused sin. Matthew 13:41. Since "all have sinned and fall short of the glory of God" (Romans 3:23), there was a time in each of our lives when we'd have fallen into that category. So the farmer was rightly concerned that the wheat would be pulled up with the tares!

In His infinite wisdom and great mercy, He did not let the servants pull the tares immediately, but waited until the wheat grows to maturity. As the children of God (the wheat) grow, they "face trials of many kinds." James 1:2. But this "testing of your faith produces perseverance." James 1:3. And once perseverance has finished its work, the children of God will be "mature and complete, not lacking anything." James 2:4. The wheat will be mature, not lacking any fruit, and they will bow before the King in reverence. Praise God that "He has not dealt with us according to our sins . . . So great is His mercy toward those who fear Him!" Psalm 103:10-11.

3.   The wheat must beware of the tares

While we wait for the harvest, the children of God—the wheat—must take care, for the tares among us are infectious. These lovers of pleasure who have the appearance of godliness are not just a danger to themselves; they are a danger to all believers. Paul told Timothy, "From such people turn away!" 2 Timothy 3:5. We should all heed these words. As Paul traveled toward Jerusalem for the last time, he called the leaders of the Ephesian church to a farewell conference. At this emotional gathering, Paul said, "I know this, that after my departure savage wolves will come in among you, not sparing the flock. Also from among yourselves men will rise up, speaking perverse things, to draw away the disciples after themselves." Acts 20:29-30. Notice that Paul warned that men would rise up "from among yourselves." From within the church. And what would they do? Draw people away after themselves. In other words, they would try to build their own kingdoms by drawing away Christ's disciples.

This warning against those who have the form of godliness without the heart is not just for the church body— it's for leaders. A little leaven can leaven the whole lump— including those in leadership. Let's be honest: those of us who preach, lead Bible studies, evangelize, etc., like it when someone tells us how good we did. But we can't fall in love with hearing it. If we do, we'll start catering our message to our admirers rather than to God. Paul warned that "the time will come when they will not endure sound doctrine, but according to their own desires, because they have itching ears, they will heap up for themselves teachers; and they will turn their ears away from the truth." 2 Timothy 4:3-4. If we fall in love with the "amens" or the crowds, we just might end up being one of those who teach only what the lovers of pleasure want to hear—a gospel that gives you a savior without requiring you to accept a King and His kingdom.

F. Recognizing the difference between the wheat and the tares

Like the parable says, the wheat and the tares are destined for much different ends. The tares are burned, while the wheat "will shine forth as the sun in the kingdom of their Father." Matthew 13:41-43. But that doesn't mean the tares are expecting this outcome. We saw in Matthew 7 that many who say "Lord, Lord" won't enter the kingdom because He never knew them. Yet they seem surprised by the outcome. How do we educate people so they don't end up being one of those many who are not known by Jesus? Let's talk about that.

1. Who is strong enough to enter the narrow gate?

How strong are you? Jesus warned, "Strive to enter through the narrow gate, for many, I say to you, will seek to enter and will not be able." Luke 13:24. Green's Literal Translation of the Bible[12] says it this way, "Labor to enter in through the narrow gate, for I say to you that many will seek to enter in and will *not have strength.*"

What does Jesus mean when He says some will not have the strength to enter? Elsewhere, Jesus expanded on this theme, saying, "the violent take [the kingdom of heaven] by force." Matthew 11:12. Jesus didn't mean that we could force our way into the kingdom against His will. Nor was Jesus talking in this verse about believers suffering persecution (though He did say plenty about that elsewhere). Instead, He was saying that those who desire to enter the kingdom of heaven will pursue their King with violent intensity. They will be zealous for their King.

So who are the ones who labor, yet do not have the

---

[12] Like Young's Literal Translation, Green's Literal Translation is another effort to translate the Bible word for word.

strength to enter in—who can't muster the passion to take the Kingdom by force? Let's look at what Jesus went on to say in Luke 13: "When once the Master of the house has risen up and shut the door, and you begin to stand outside and knock at the door, saying, 'Lord, Lord, open for us,' and He will answer and say to you, 'I do not know you, where you are from.'" Luke 13:25.

What? Jesus just said that He did not know these people! These people are seeking, yet are not allowed in. What should that tell us? In being seeker-friendly, we can't neglect to proclaim the full counsel of God, "Repent, for the kingdom of God is at hand." It's great to be welcoming, but we can't give those seekers the idea that "seeking" is a state of peace with God. It's a state of peril!

Let's see how the seekers in Luke 13 respond to Jesus— maybe those who don't have the strength to enter will be able to talk their way in. Instead, they reply to Jesus by saying, "We ate and drank in Your presence, and You taught in our streets." Luke 13:26. This sounds pretty good, right? They hung out with Jesus—they ate with Him; they heard His teaching. But it turns out that's not enough. He says, "I tell you I do not know you, where you are from. Depart from Me all you workers of iniquity." Luke 13:27. Where do they depart to? He says they will be "thrust out" to a place where "there will be weeping and gnashing of teeth." Luke 13:27-28.

"Thrust out" is very strong language. Remember, Jesus is talking about people who have been in His presence. They had an encounter with Him. Maybe they held up their hands during worship. Maybe they made a lot of noise. Maybe they even sobbed uncontrollably. But Jesus' response is that He does not know them. They will be "thrust out" of His kingdom to that place of weeping and gnashing of teeth. So I ask again: who are these people who heard Jesus' teaching and ate with Him, without ever letting Him get to know them?

Here's the answer: The ones that Jesus never knows are those who love God for all that He has done, is doing, and will do, but never fall in love with Him.

2.   It's not enough to love His sacrifice

Many say they love God because His Son died for them. Ok, but if that's the reason we should love Him, then did anyone in the Old Testament (say, Abraham, Moses, or David) love God? They didn't have a full appreciation for the coming sacrifice God would make, so how could they have loved God—if Jesus' death is the main reason we should love Him? The answer: that's not the main reason we should love Jesus. While Jesus' death is an amazing sacrifice, we must love Him who was sacrificed, not just His act of sacrifice. Many love God's riches and power, yet don't love Him who owns the riches and the power. When you love who He is, you will love what He has done, is doing, and will do. But you can love what He has done, is doing, and will do without actually loving Him.

Job is a great example of someone who loved God because He is God, rather than because of all that He has. When the book of Job opens, Job is a very wealthy man with ten kids he loves. Then, in a handful of minutes, Job loses everything—the fruits of all his life and labor. If you've read the story, you know that God ends up restoring Job's wealth and blessing him with ten more children.[13] But remember that Job didn't know the end of the story at the beginning or in the middle. All he knew was that disaster had struck hard and fast. Imagine yourself sitting there at age 60, with everything looking like you're going to cruise into retirement

---

[13] This isn't to say that Job's first ten children were "replaced" by the second ten. But given how Job trusted God with his kids in this life, do you think he trusted God to take care of them after this life?

a wealthy man, when you suddenly get a series of messages saying that you lost your job, your retirement fund was embezzled, your house burned down (and you forgot to renew your insurance), and, by the way, all your kids died. That's what happened to Job.

How did Job react? He said, "Naked I came from my mother's womb, and naked shall I return there. The LORD gave, and the LORD has taken away; Blessed be the name of the LORD." Job 1:21. Wow! Is that how we would respond to those disasters? And don't mistake Job's reaction to mean that he didn't care—Job also tore his robe and shaved his head. But, most importantly, he worshiped. Job 1:20.

I think we can agree that Job loved God. And Job loved God not just for the benefits to Job; He loved God for who He is—the great I AM. Job's worshipful response was immediate. It was his heartfelt reaction. He was not just saying what he was supposed to say.

How do you think God felt when He heard Job's response? Do we now understand why God said, "Have you considered my servant Job, that there is none like him on the earth, a blameless and upright man, one who fears God and shuns evil?" Job 1:8. Wouldn't that be good to hear God say?

The book of Daniel gives us another great illustration of men who loved God for being God. In Daniel 3, we read about three Jewish men, Shadrach, Meshach, and Abed-Nego, who lived during Israel's captivity in Babylon. These three men had been put in charge of Babylon by King Nebuchadnezzar. Daniel 2:49. I'm sure their jobs came with plenty of benefits, but one day they also came with a downside: an order to bow down to a golden idol that Nebuchadnezzar had constructed. Daniel 3:1-12.

They had to choose whether to bow down or stand before

this false god. At the same time, they were choosing whether to bow down or stand before the true God. They couldn't do both. To bow before one was to stand before the other. To honor the false god (and everything it represented—wealth, power, position, control, etc.) was to deny the true God. Are things so different today? Don't we all make this same decision about who or what we will bow before?

Shadrach, Meshach, and Abed-Nego would not bow down. They stood their ground even under the threat of death by being thrown into a fiery furnace. They said to the king, "O Nebuchadnezzar, we have no need to answer you in this matter." Daniel 3:16. They had no need to answer Nebuchadnezzar because, while the Bible instructs us to honor earthly authorities, when it comes to who we bow before, we answer only to God. They trusted that if Nebuchadnezzar threw them in the fiery furnace, God would save them: "Our God whom we serve is able to deliver us from the burning fiery furnace, and He will deliver us from your hand, O king." Daniel 3:17. Look at that faith!

But here's how you know they loved God for God, not just for what He can do in this world. They didn't stop by saying they believed God would save them. They went on to explain that even if He didn't save them, they would still choose God: "But if not [that is, if God does not save us from the furnace], let it be known to you, O king, that we do not serve your gods, nor will we worship the gold image which you have set up." Daniel 3:18. Wow! Amen! In other words, "we don't love God just because He can pull us out of every bad situation in this world. We love Him because He's God." Like these three men, we need to fall in love with God because He's God.

To fall in love with God, we must do more than love what He loves—we can do that while still wanting to be our own king. Instead of ceding everything to Him, we try to create an alliance with God to bring our desires to pass. It's like saying, "Ok, God, You have Your kingdom and I'll have my kingdom. But I know You have a lot of resources, so I'd like to team up with you to build up my kingdom."

Unfortunately for our personal kingdoms, that's not how God works. To accept His kingship, we must accept His full agenda. That means we not only have to love what He loves, but also hate what He hates. God says, "Hate evil, love good; establish justice in the gate." Amos 5:15. Paul even suggests that hating what God hates is a necessary counterpart to genuine love: "Let love be genuine. Abhor what is evil; hold fast to what is good." Romans 12:9 (ESV). One thing He hates is our kingships—He will see that they are all destroyed. As Paul said, Jesus will put "an end to all rule and all authority and all power." 1 Corinthians 15:24. Our kingdom can either be destroyed through us submitting to peace on His terms (not ours) or through war. We're a lot better off if we choose peace.

G. Why a King

We've learned that the sin is the desire to be our own king. Lucifer was the first to act on this desire. Then Adam followed his wife Eve in succumbing to "the sin". Through Adam, "the sin" and "the death" entered the world. One man wanted to be king, and from his choice "the sin" and "the death" came to us all. The sad thing is, he had already been given dominion by God, but apparently wasn't content with that.

Mankind became captive to "the sin". Paul tells us that "the sin" is a law unto itself, a law against God (and, therefore, it is lawlessness). Paul tells us that we are captives to "the sin": "I behold another law in my members, warring against the law of my mind, and bringing me into captivity to the law of the sin that [is] in my members." Romans 7:24. After summarizing mankind's slavery to "the sin", Paul ends with this lament and cry for help on behalf of man: "A wretched man I [am]! Who shall deliver me out of the body of this death?" Romans 7:24 (YLT).

With Paul's question in mind—"who shall deliver me out of the body of this death" that results from our desire to be king—let's re-read John 1:29. It will help us understand the full impact of what John the Baptist was saying. "The next day John saw Jesus coming toward him, and said, 'Behold! The Lamb of God who takes away *the sin* of the world!'" John 1:29.

Jesus Christ is the one who takes away "the sin", that desire to be our own king. Without Him, we are slaves to "the sin". Jesus delivers us from our god complex. He destroys the power of it. It's only in this way that we can "deny [ourselves], take up [our] cross daily, and follow [Him]." Luke 9:23. That's why Paul answers his own question, "Who shall deliver me out of the body of this death?" He goes on to say,

"I thank God—through Jesus Christ our Lord . . . for the law of the Spirit of the life in Christ Jesus did set me free from the law of *the sin* and of the death." Romans 7:24-8:2 (YLT). Without the King coming to destroy our kingship, we would climb right back onto that throne. That is why Jesus started His earthly ministry by proclaiming, "Repent, for the Kingdom of God is at hand." Matthew 4:17. He wanted man (and woman) to surrender his desire to have his own kingdom, and to receive His Kingdom.

Jesus makes us a new creation. The new creation isn't trying to make a name for ourselves anymore; the new creation has a heart to exercise dominion in His name. That's why Jesus came. That's why John called Jesus the Lamb of God who takes away *the* sin of the world, not "the sins" of the world. John understood that Jesus came to take away *the* sin, and that by doing so, He effectively dealt with our "sins" problem, as well. By changing the root, He also changes the fruit.

1.   Healing the root instead of picking the fruit

Every fruit on a tree comes from a root. It's critical to understand the difference between the root (the sin) and the fruit (all the sins that *the* sin leads to). All sins point back to the root. Take lying, for example. I think we'd all agree that it's generally a sin. But why do we lie? We lie to protect ourselves—our own kingdom. When someone steals, it is to benefit himself or his interest. Lust is wanting something for self-gratification. And it's the same with all the many other sins we could list. People commit those sins in furtherance of *the* sin—to advance the interests of their personal kingdom.

Let's say you have a tree growing poisonous fruit. You want to deal with it. What do you do? If you remove the fruit, you address the problem for a while. But more fruit will grow back. And it will still be poisonous because you didn't deal with the root. If you want to change the fruit, you have to change the root.

Many of us have been told that we need Jesus to take away our sins (fruit). That's factual, but it doesn't capture the truth that Jesus wants to heal our sins by healing the root—the sin. Healing our sins, the fruit, is not a permanent solution. We can ask for help in dealing with the fruit (say, pornography, gossip, or gluttony), but if that's all we ask for, we're not healing the root. We haven't sought His kingdom and fallen in love with Him and His culture. We haven't said, "Not my will, but Your will be done." We haven't surrendered our kingship to Him.

Many of us just ask Him to fix the problems our kingship created so we can continue running our kingdom—into the ground. If we do that, we're going to continue to grow poisonous fruit, often without realizing why this is happening. We might exchange one sin for another, but it won't be healthy fruit. If we want to get rid of the bad fruit, we have to heal the root. Heal the root, and there will be new fruit.

We all have to get our root healed to avoid the death— eternal death. Look back to Romans 5:12 (YLT): "even as through one man *the* sin did enter into the world, and through *the* sin the death; and thus to all men the death did pass through, for that *all* did sin." See that—all have sinned. And when I say all, I mean all. David wrote, "Surely I was born a sinner yes, from the moment my mother conceived me." Psalm 51:5.

I always wondered how a baby could be considered a sinner if the child never did any sin. An infant seems so innocent; how could she be capable of sinning? Then, when I began to understand *the* sin and how every root produces a fruit, I was able to really receive God's word that all are sinners. It's not a matter of whether we are going to commit sinful deeds, it is just a matter of when. Each one of us is born with the root—the sin, the desire to be our own king—and, without the benefit of Christ's work, we will always bear sinful fruit.

2.   The new root grows from seed—the Word of the kingdom

We're all born with a bad root—the sin. We know Jesus can deliver us, but how? How do new roots grow? From seed.

Jesus provides the seed that grows our new root. Jesus said, "The kingdom of heaven is like a mustard seed, which a man took and sowed in his field, which indeed is the least of all the seeds; but when it is grown it is greater than the herbs and becomes a tree, so that the birds of the air come and nest in its branches." Matthew 13:31-32. To get a fuller understanding of what Jesus meant in comparing the Kingdom of Heaven to a mustard seed, consider that Young's Literal Translation of these verses uses the word "reign" instead of "kingdom." So the reign of heaven is like a mustard seed that replaces the old seed—the reign of man.

To carry this a little further, think about another parable about sowing seed recorded in Matthew 13. In this parable, Jesus said that the seed is the Word of the Kingdom (that is, the reign of heaven). The seed is sown in fields, which are the hearts of men. In many, the seed will not grow to bear fruit because (1) they don't understand the Word and the devil steals it; (2) they let the cares of the world choke out the Word; or (3) the Word does not take solid root and trouble or persecution causes them to fall away.

But as for those who hear the Word and understand it, their hearts are good soil. The seed—the Word of the

Kingdom, the reign of Heaven—takes good root in their hearts. And, with patience, the reign of Heaven grows and they bear good fruit, some thirtyfold, some sixtyfold, and some a hundredfold. Matthew 13:23; Luke 8:15.

Remember that Jesus came to preach the Gospel—the Good News—of the Kingdom. The Word become flesh came to preach the word of the Kingdom—His Kingdom. Jesus came to proclaim His kingdom because He is the King of kings. That doesn't just mean that Jesus is King over what we usually think of as earthly kingdoms like the Roman empire, China, or the United States. In coming as King, Jesus also proclaimed His reign over the individual kingdoms of our lives.

3.   Who considers the Gospel to be good news?

Some might wonder why the kingdom of God is called the "good news" (that is, the gospel). Why is it good news that Jesus came to take us off our thrones? Not many kings would see the good news in a stronger king showing up to dethrone them. Just ask King Herod, king over Israel when Jesus was born.

When wise men from the east came to Jerusalem, asking, "Where is He who has been born king of the Jews," Herod was "troubled." Matthew 2:3. That was putting it mildly— when Herod couldn't track down the one who had been born king of the Jews, he killed all the boys two years old and under in the region of Bethlehem. He didn't choose Bethlehem randomly—he killed all the little boys in that region because that's where he heard the Messiah was to be born. Herod demonstrates just how far a king will go to hang on to his throne—he will knowingly try to kill the anointed One of God.

So maybe the Kingdom of God is not good news in the

eyes of everyone. It is good news to those who are poor in spirit, those who realize that God is "I AM" and they "are not." But the Kingdom of God is good news to God. That captures the point of this book—the Bible is about God, not man. If we can accept that, we will step out of a vain conversation and into a God conversation. We will start to love what He loves and hate what He hates.

V.   The Gospel: Fulfilling God's Desire

God has a desire He will see come to pass. Paul talks about it in Ephesians, calling it "the mystery of His will." Ephesians 1:9. What is the mystery of God's will? That, "according to His purpose, which he set forth in Christ as a plan for the fullness of time, to unite all things in him, things in heaven and on earth." Ephesians 1:9-10.

I know that's a mouthful. So I summarize it like this: God's desire is to see Heaven invade earth. Sometimes I get weird looks when I say that. It's true, though! Remember what Jesus taught us to pray: "Our Father in heaven, hallowed be your name. Your kingdom come, your will be done, on earth as it is in heaven." Matthew 6:9-10 (ESV). Do you see that? Jesus told us to pray that the Father's Kingdom come on earth. That is His will. That is His dream.

God's will—His dream—will indeed come to pass. The Kingdom comes in full after our Lord Jesus Christ returns. The prophet Daniel saw a vision of "One like the Son of Man . . . [who] was given dominion and glory and a kingdom, that all peoples, nations, and languages should serve Him. His dominion is an everlasting dominion, which shall not pass away, and His kingdom the one which shall not be destroyed." Daniel 7:13-14. He will establish the Kingdom "with judgment and justice from that time forward, even forever. The zeal of the LORD of hosts will perform this." Isaiah 9:7. For those who continue in the faith, "there will be richly provided for you an entrance into the eternal kingdom of our Lord and Savior Jesus Christ." 2 Peter 1:10-11 (ESV); *see also* Acts 14:22. Come, Lord Jesus, come!

But Scripture tells us that the Kingdom is here even now. In Daniel 2, Daniel interprets a dream for King Nebuchadnezzar. In that dream, God showed King Nebuchadnezzar four kingdoms, which pretty much everyone agrees refer to the neo-Babylonian, Greek, Medo-Persian, and Roman empires. Then, Daniel says that "in the days of those kings the God of heaven will set up a kingdom that shall never be destroyed, nor shall the kingdom be left to another people." Daniel 2:44 (ESV). Notice that God sets up this eternal Kingdom in the days of those kings described in Daniel 2, which conclude with the Roman empire—the dominant world power that controlled Israel during Jesus' ministry. That means the eternal Kingdom went into effect during that time.

Remember that Jesus and John the Baptist said, "Repent, for the kingdom of heaven is *at hand*." They really meant it. The Kingdom was at hand right then. When the Pharisees asked Jesus when the kingdom of God would come, Jesus didn't say, "It won't come for at least a couple thousand years." Instead, He told them, "The kingdom of God is not coming in ways that can be observed." Luke 17:20 (ESV). He said, "the kingdom of God is in the midst of you." Luke 17:21 (ESV). So, while it's not apparent to the world, the Kingdom of God is in the midst of us who are poor in spirit even now!

If you're struggling to reconcile the future kingdom with the present kingdom, remember that the word "kingdom" refers to both the king's reign over physical territory and his reign over the hearts of his people. The day will come when we physically see Jesus exercising His reign over the earth. But even now, He is exercising His reign in the hearts of those who believe. Remember that believers are now citizens of His Kingdom (Ephesians 2:19), which means that we are "sojourners and exiles" in this world. 1 Peter 2:11. That's because we can't take citizenship in God's Kingdom while maintaining citizenship in Satan's domain, where our personal kingdoms reside.

Not only do we become citizens of God's Kingdom, we

play a role in the government of His Kingdom even today. Specifically, we serve as "ambassadors for Christ." 2 Corinthians 5:20. This position we hold demonstrates His current reign over us—an ambassador serves the interest of his sovereign authority. As evidence of His present reign in our hearts, we who believe have been "sealed with the Holy Spirit of promise, who is the guarantee of our inheritance until the redemption of the purchased possession, to the praise of His glory." Ephesians 1:13-14.

That brings us to an important point. God wants your heart. He wants it so badly that He's at war for it. Who is He warring against? The devil—and us. Remember, you're either under Satan's authority or you've been conveyed into God's Kingdom. We're under one or the other. God wants us in His Kingdom. But we can't be citizens of His Kingdom while we're in the devil's kingdom.

So what has to happen? Jesus said, "The time has come. . . . The kingdom of God has come near. Repent and believe the good news!" Matthew 4:17 (NIV). In other words, we have to repent of trying to sit on His throne. To "repent" doesn't just mean saying "sorry" for being your own king—it means doing something about it. It means turning away from your kingdom, which resides squarely in the middle of Satan's territory. To gain citizenship in God's Kingdom, we must renounce citizenship in our kingdom.

We must stage an insurrection against Satan's rule. Adam came underneath Satan's rule by rebelling against God, and all mankind has followed his lead. Now, we must stage another rebellion. This rebellion takes place within our heart. We reject ourselves and our way—the desire to be king. We throw open the gates of our heart and invite the King to invade. And so He does, destroying the works of the devil. 1 John 3:8.

Jesus told us about this. Near the end of His earthly ministry, Jesus said, "Now the ruler of this world will be cast out." John 12:31. But what does that mean? We know that even after Jesus ascended back to the right hand of the Father, Paul referred to Satan as the ruler of this world and the god of this age. That sure sounds like Satan still has authority in this world. So where did the ruler of this world get cast out from?

Satan has been cast out from the hearts of those who repent and invite in the true King. As Paul writes, "We are the temple of the living God. . . . What harmony can there be between Christ and the devil?" 2 Corinthians 6:16 (NLT). When we welcome His Kingdom by throwing open the kingdom of our hearts, we begin to fulfill God's dream that the Kingdom of Heaven will invade earth. I hope that the thought of fulfilling God's dream excites you as much as it does me!

A.   The Penalty for Treason is Death

But that still leaves a problem to overcome. And it's a big one. I said that we have to throw open the gates of our kingdom to Jesus. But remember that God has always been the rightful owner of the throne of our hearts. No matter how old we are when we come to Christ, we've already tried to steal His throne. So when we open our kingdom to Him, we stand before Him guilty of treason.

What usually happens when an earthly king conquers someone trying to steal his throne? The penalty for treason is death. And indeed, when Jesus comes at the end of the age, He will strike down the kings of the nations (Revelation 19:17-21), just as Psalm 2 warned thousands of years in advance. That doesn't seem to bode well for all of us would-be kings.

But striking us all down for treason would not fulfill God's dream. He "is longsuffering toward us, not willing that any should perish but that all should come to repentance." 2 Peter 3:9. God so loved the world that He didn't let our treason stop His plan. He is a God of mercy, and provided a way for us pretenders to the throne to enter His Kingdom.

God told us the way long before Jesus walked the earth. Through Isaiah the prophet, God said, "Seek the Lord while He may be found. Call upon Him while He is near." Isaiah 55:6. What does it mean to seek the Lord? "Let the wicked forsake his way, and the unrighteous man his thoughts." Isaiah 55:7. Now look at the promise God makes to the one who returns to Him: "He will have mercy on Him. . . . He will abundantly pardon." Isaiah 55:7. What God offers is just what we need: a pardon for our treason.

But don't think He simply overlooked our capital crimes. He is a God of justice, and justice demands a price for crime.

The penalty for our treason is death—including eternal separation from God. Paul said we were all dead in our trespasses (Eph. 2:1), and Jesus said that God is "not God of the dead, but of the living." Mark 12:27. So how could we ever enter the kingdom of God?

1. Jesus' work on the cross provides access to the kingdom

You and I have no access to the Kingdom without that which is of first importance—what Christ did for us through His obedience to the Father. Jesus' 3½-year work was completed by the 3-day work. To seek the Kingdom without the death and resurrection of our Lord would be of no effect.

In fact, Paul says that even attempting to do that separates us from Christ: "You have become estranged from Christ, you who attempt to be justified by the law; you have fallen from grace." Galatians 5:4. When we remember that it is only "by grace you have been saved through faith," we understand the gravity of Paul's warning against falling from grace by trying to justify ourselves by doing good things. Ephesians 2:8. If we're relying on anything we do to enter the Kingdom, we will end up weeping and gnashing our teeth along with everyone else who loved the lie that they could rely on their own righteousness.

But why couldn't Jesus just come as King? Why did He have to die to bring heaven to earth? Actually, He didn't have to die to bring heaven to earth. He had to die to allow us to be part of it. The Father made it possible to fulfill His plan of salvation through the ultimate sacrifice—the life of His Son, Jesus Christ. The One without sin. The Lamb without blemish. God "made Him who knew no sin to be sin for us, that we might become the righteousness of God in Him." 2 Corinthians 5:21.

The work of the cross was the bridge that connected heaven to earth. The bottom of the cross placed in the earth and the top of the cross placed in heaven. And on it was God in flesh, simultaneously the Son of God and the Son of Man, connecting the two realms together. John 1:51; Genesis 28:15. The Gospel is the Good News of the Kingdom of God, and Jesus' work on the cross provides access to enter the Kingdom of Heaven while on earth.

Stated another way, Jesus said, "I am the door." John 10:9. After His resurrection, Jesus said that He "has the key of David." Revelation 3:7. What does that mean? Remember what the angel Gabriel told Mary, the mother of Jesus about her Son: "the Lord God will give Him the throne of His father David . . . and of His kingdom there will be no end." Luke 1:32-33. The work of the cross gave Jesus the key to the Kingdom. He is the One "who opens and no one will shut, who shuts and no one opens." Revelation 3:7.

2.   To receive the benefit of the cross, we must follow the path Jesus described

The Gospel is the good news of the Kingdom of God, but it's only good news if you're able to receive it. Remember the parable of the sower: those who did not understand the word of the Kingdom had it snatched away by the devil. Matthew 13:19. Paul says that the devil blinds those who don't understand—they cannot see the light of the Gospel of Christ. 2 Corinthians 4:3-5. So the devil makes sure that those who don't understand won't understand and be saved by seeing the glory—the inherent, infinite splendor of Christ. Matthew 13:19; Luke 8:12.

But if the Gospel is only good news to those who receive it, how do we receive it? Let's start with an analogy. When we contemplate marriage, there are certain benefits we expect to come along with it. But are we supposed to consummate the marriage before the marriage occurs? Or is there some sowing to do before we reap the fruit?

If you've made it this far into this book, I hope you agree that there is a proper order! We carefully contemplate whether this is the right person to enter into a one-flesh, till-death-do-us part relationship. If we decide yes, then we enter into that covenant before God and the relevant governmental authority. Only then do we consummate the marriage. Many of us do start with consummation before contemplation and covenant. Sometimes things eventually work out anyway. But our failure to follow God's plan usually leads to a lot of unnecessary pain and confusion.

Similarly, we must follow the path that Jesus described in order to form the relationship He desires. And even though our human nature wants to receive the benefit of the cross upfront, just like with marriage, that's not how Jesus said it works. While some who start out by seeking the benefits of Jesus will eventually develop a true relationship with Him, it often involves a lot of pain. And some who start out by seeking His benefits never do find Him.

With that in mind, we're going to look at the path Jesus laid out for us: (1) seeking the Kingdom of God and His righteousness; (2) counting the cost; and (3) receiving that which is of first importance—Christ Jesus and His work. We'll examine each of these in a bit, but I want to start with an example of a woman who walked this path beautifully—even though she lived more than a thousand years before Mary gave birth to Jesus. We would do well to follow her example.

3.   Rahab shows us how it's done

Let me tell you about Rahab—this woman understood what it meant to seek God's Kingdom, counting the cost along the way. And, after doing so, she came into His Kingdom. We first hear about her in Joshua 2, just after the death of Moses, as Joshua prepares to lead the Israelites in their conquest of the promised land. The first major city facing them was Jericho, a heavily fortified city. Joshua sent two men into the land to spy it out in preparation for the Israelites' invasion. They lodged at the house of a prostitute—Rahab. Joshua 2:1.

Rahab was quickly faced with a decision. The king of Jericho learned that the Israelite spies were in the city. Not only that, he knew they entered the house of Rahab. He sent to her, demanding that she bring them out to the king. Joshua 2:2-3. What was Rahab to do? Normally, this would have been an easy choice. When the king asks you to turn over spies, you turn over the spies. To do otherwise amounts to treason.

But Rahab had received a critical revelation. The people of Jericho had heard what God had already done for the Israelites, including their destruction of two nearby Amorite kingdoms. As a result, Rahab said, "Our hearts melted, and there was no spirit left in any man because of you." Joshua 2:11. But Rahab's revelation went a step further. She understood that "the LORD your God, he is God in the heavens above and on the earth beneath." Joshua 2:11.

This revelation made what normally would have been an easy decision for Rahab a life-determining test of faith. Rahab had to decide which kingdom she would seek. The king of Jericho could kill her for her treason if she hid the Israelite spies. But since she believed that God had given Jericho to the Israelites, what value remained in protecting her place in her land? She might have asked herself, "What will it profit me if I gain the whole world, yet forfeit my soul?" See Matthew 16:26 (ESV).

Rahab threw open the gates of her heart and, in a sense, the gates of her actual kingdom, by revealing the fear of her people. Rahab decided to seek God's Kingdom instead of the kingdom of Jericho. In doing so, Rahab gives us a preview of what Jesus meant 1,500 years later when He said, "Do not fear those who kill the body but cannot kill the soul. But rather fear Him who is able to destroy both soul and body in hell." Mathew 10:28. Rahab protected the spies, asking them to show her mercy when Israel conquered the city. Joshua 2:12. So they did, and she and her relatives were delivered from the destruction that soon came upon Jericho. Joshua 6:22-25.

Rahab counted the cost in throwing open the gates of her heart. The decision wasn't forced on her. She had the opportunity to choose her earthly kingdom. When the king's men showed up at her door asking about the spies, she had the chance to say, "I have no king but Caesar." But she decided to make herself an exile—an outsider—in the kingdom of Jericho. Sure, she remained physically present in that kingdom a little while longer, but that's not where her heart was. She chose the unknown over the known.

If she had longed for Jericho, she had the opportunity to change her mind. The Israelite spies spent the night at her house, so she could have gone to the king and given them up. But Rahab was looking forward to a better kingdom. She chose the Kingdom of the King she had never seen over the kingdom she knew. Maybe she looked around and saw where seeking her kingdom had led her—into prostitution. What could the king of Jericho take away from her? Her place as a prostitute? She chose the Kingdom of the King she rightly feared.

What was the difference between Rahab and the rest of Jericho? After all, she said that there was no spirit left in *any* man in the city because of the Lord. Joshua 2:11. According to Rahab, all Jericho was grieving, so why didn't all Jericho seek the mercy of the Lord? I think we find an answer in Paul's second letter to the Corinthians, where Paul identifies two very different types of grief: (1) worldly grief that produces death; and (2) Godly grief that produces repentance. 2 Corinthians 7:10.

Jericho exhibited worldly grief. Their hearts melted before the judgment of the Lord, but it did not lead them to throw open the gates for Him. When the Israelites showed up, "Jericho was shut up inside and outside." Joshua 6:1. They barred their physical gates, as well as the gates of their hearts, against Yahweh God. Their kingdom could not stand against God, however, and the walls of Jericho came tumbling down. And so will the kingdoms of all who refuse to throw open the gates of their hearts.

In contrast, Rahab demonstrated the Godly grief that leads to repentance. In the New Testament, Rahab received praised for the faith she showed through her actions: "By faith Rahab the prostitute did not perish with those who were disobedient, because she had given a friendly welcome to the spies." Hebrews 11:31. Having sought the Kingdom of God and counted the cost, Rahab received the tender mercies of the King. The King brought her into His Kingdom. He restored the prostitute, making her a wife. And not only a wife, but a (grand)mother of Jesus.

What do you think occupied the thoughts of the Son of God as He looked down on Rahab? Do you think He focused on her acts of prostitution? He had seen many acts of prostitution; I doubt that drew His attention. She was a prostitute among a people of prostitutes. Why would He focus on her harlotry when the men of her city went aside with harlots? Hosea 4:14. I don't think He focused on her prostitution, but that she was poor in spirit and wanted out of her kingdom and into His. I think He saw that her faith was in Him, no longer was her faith in her kingdom.

The Bible tells us that "without faith it is impossible to please [God], for he who comes to God must believe that He is, and that He is a rewarder of those who diligently seek Him." Hebrews 11:6. How much do you think the faith of Rahab pleased Him? I imagine the Son turned to the Father and said, "Father, do you see the faith of Rahab!?" I think the Son said, "Father, I desire that she would be with Me where I am, that she would see Me in My glory!" See John 17:24. And I think the Father said, "I see her faith, My Son. I will give You the desire of Your heart." See John 5:20-21.

Rahab's faith was counted to her as righteousness. James 2:21-25. All those acts of prostitution? As far as the east is from the west, so did He remove her transgressions from her. Psalm 103:12. The prostitute was purified by Him in whom she hoped. 1 John 3:3. The sullied prostitute walked in white garments.

What was Rahab's part in this redemption she experienced? She sought the Kingdom of God and His righteousness, counting the cost—forsaking the old kingdom, the good and the bad alike. When she did, she received citizenship in His Kingdom. Now let's talk about what that looks like in our lives.

B.   Seeking First the Kingdom of God and His Righteousness

Jesus said, "Seek first the kingdom of God and His righteousness." Matthew 6:33 (ESV). How does someone go about seeking the Kingdom of God (that is, the King and His culture) and His righteousness? Someone could start by listing a bunch of things the King likes and try to do them. But would that get him anywhere? Isn't that what the Bible tells us is futile? We'll never do good enough to justify ourselves before God. Paul says, "None is righteous." Romans 3:10 (ESV). In fact, "our unrighteousness serves to show the righteousness of God." Romans 3:5 (ESV).

So how will we find the King and His culture—the righteousness of God? Paul gives us insight in Romans 3. He says, "The righteousness of God has been manifested apart from the law." That's the way it had to be, since we're never going to be justified by our own good deeds. How can one be justified by his good deeds if he is still sitting on a throne that never belonged to him? It does not matter how good someone thinks he's doing if he is committing treason. Ephesians 2:8 (ESV). Instead, God put forward Jesus "as a propitiation by His blood, to be received by faith." Romans 3:25 (ESV). Look what comes next: "This was to show God's righteousness." Romans 3:25 (ESV). How does Jesus' shed blood show God's righteousness? Because Jesus' blood allows God to show mercy to us without foregoing the judgment we deserve. Jesus' sacrifice allows God to "be just and the justifier of the one who has faith in Jesus." Romans 3:26 (ESV).

So what does it mean to seek the righteousness of God? Paul says that while the Law and the Prophets bear witness to it, the righteousness of God has now been revealed: "the righteousness of God through the faithfulness of Jesus Christ for all who believe." Romans 3:21 (NET). In other words, the

164

righteousness of God comes via one path—Christ and Him crucified. 1 Corinthians 2:2. "For our sake he made him to be sin who knew no sin, so that in him we might become the righteousness of God." 2 Corinthians 5:21 (ESV).

Remember that "the sin" is lawlessness (1 John 3:4 (YLT)), and that *the* sin is the desire to be our own king. When we think of it like that, it's no surprise that righteousness has no partnership with lawlessness. 2 Corinthians 6:14. We can't find the righteousness of God, the Christ, the King, while living the sin—the desire to be our own king, committing treason. And since the only way to become the righteousness of God is by finding the King and His culture, we have to leave behind our kingdom (our kingship and our culture).

Once we become the righteousness of God through faith in Christ, we can (and should) practice righteousness (1 John 3:7) because "the fruit of righteousness comes through Christ." Philippians 1:11 (ESV). Paul twice told Timothy to flee from examples of unrighteousness (including the love of money and youthful passions) and instead to "pursue righteousness." 1 Timothy 6:11; 2 Timothy 2:22. In both passages, Paul tells Timothy to pursue other characteristics along with righteousness, such as faith, love, peace, gentleness, and steadfastness, but in both instances, Paul says to that the pursuit begins with righteousness.

Paul expands on this theme in Ephesians, framing the pursuit of righteousness as the proper response to delivery from vain conversation: "Now this I say and testify in the Lord, that you must no longer walk as the Gentiles do, in the futility [or vanity (KJV)] of their minds." Ephesians 4:17 (ESV). Paul is explaining that those who live a vain conversation (that is, a futile way of life) are "alienated from the life of God because of the ignorance that is in them, due to their hardness of heart." Ephesians 4:18. What is the result? Unrighteous behavior—they "become callous and have given themselves up to sensuality, greedy to practice every kind of impurity." Ephesians 4:19 (ESV).

But in Christ that's who we were, not who we are! Paul distinguishes believers from those still living a vain conversation, zeroing in on the pursuit of righteousness that we begin after becoming the righteousness of God. When we put our faith in Christ, we "put off [our] old self, which . . . is corrupt through deceitful desires." Ephesians 4:22 (ESV). We put off that old self because it "belongs to [our] former manner of life," that is, our vain conversation. Ephesians 4:21-22 (ESV). As believers, we are "renewed in the spirit of [our] minds." Ephesians 4:23 (ESV). We "put on the new self, created after the likeness of God in true righteousness and holiness." Ephesians 4:24 (ESV). That new self created after the likeness of God will display the fruits of the Spirit: "love, joy, peace, longsuffering, kindness, goodness, faithfulness, gentleness, self-control." Galatians 5:22-23.

So how do we seek the King and His culture, His righteousness? It goes back to setting aside our own kingship and our own culture, and seeking after Christ's. Putting aside our own opinions on what we love and what we hate and instead being willing to put on the mind of Christ, loving what He loves and hating what He hates.

This makes sense when we remember who the Kingdom is for. Jesus said, "Blessed are the poor in spirit, for theirs is the kingdom of heaven." Matthew 5:3. Who are the poor in spirit? Those who realize they "are not," so they seek the One who is I AM. Those who no longer desire to be the king of their lives. And understand, being poor in spirit isn't just a moment in time. It's a lifestyle. The poor in spirit want to get out of *the* sin and be delivered from their own reign. They do not want to receive a "bailout" from God so they can keep living the way they were living. They fall in love with the King and His culture. They desire His eternal reign.

These poor in spirit believe the prayer that Jesus taught them will be answered: "Your kingdom come, Your will be done, on earth as it is in heaven." Matthew 6:10. They believe that the Kingdom of God will come into them as a new seed (replacing the old seed), take root, and (in time) bear the fruit of the Heavenly Kingdom.

Since the poor in spirit desire Jesus' reign, they don't sit back and wait for His Kingdom to come to them. They follow Jesus' instruction to "seek first the kingdom of God and His righteousness." Matthew 6:33. They seek the King and His culture. Jesus said, "Seek, and you will find." Matthew 7:7. But think about what that means: to seek His Kingdom, we have to leave our own kingdom, which sits squarely in Satan's territory. That means we have to let go of some things that we might have picked up while we resided there.

1.   **Seeking His righteousness means turning over the will of our hearts to Him**

In Section III(B), I asked whether it's possible that salvation might involve letting go of our own will and entering into God's will. I hope that by now you've decided it does. If we're going to surrender the kingdom of our heart to Jesus, we will first have to give up the idea of following our own heart. That's because "the human heart is the most deceitful of all things, and desperately wicked." Jeremiah 17:9 (NLT). Or, as Jesus said, "out of the heart come evil thoughts, murder, adultery, sexual immorality, theft, false witness, slander." Matthew 15:18-19.

That runs counter to how Western culture views itself, and maybe even how we view ourselves. Even in our deepest sin, few of us would have openly admitted that our hearts were desperately wicked. How often do we hear the adulterer and adulteress justify their behavior? Like them, most of us would have said something like, "I'm not that bad. I don't get up in the morning intending to do evil." Some of us could even point to some nice things that we did for other people. Yet, deep down, unless we were just too abandoned to sin to admit it anymore, we knew we did wrong all the time, even things we didn't want to do. We just couldn't help it. Why?

To frame this conversation, consider that Satan worshippers follow this creed: "Do what thou wilt shall be the whole of the law." That probably sounds really bad since I already told you it's the motto of Satan worshippers. But what if I simply rephrased it like this: "Follow your heart." Have you ever heard that? Have you ever said that?

Google "follow your heart" and check out all the Hallmark-card-style images you find with that phrase. You'll even find Steve Jobs, a man idolized in our world today, saying "Don't be trapped by dogma . . . follow your heart and intuition." But the problem is that, unless we're born again, even our "mind and conscience are defiled." Titus 1:15.

Wait until I tell you what Steve Jobs said next: "[Your heart and intuition] somehow already know what you truly want to become. Everything else is secondary." How prophetic! Just like Lucifer, your heart and intuition (that is, conscience) know what you want to become—king!

We all had *the* sin—the desire to be like God—just like Lucifer did. Everything else truly is secondary to our defiled hearts. Moses had a dire warning for the man "who . . . blesses himself in his heart, saying, 'I shall be safe, though I walk in the stubbornness of my heart.'" Deuteronomy 29:19. Moses told that man, "The LORD will not be willing to forgive him, but rather the anger of the Lord and his jealousy will smoke against that man." Deuteronomy 29:20. If someone tries to walk in the stubbornness of his heart, it means he hasn't turned his heart over to God. He still has "a root bearing bitterness." Deuteronomy 29:18.

But that's not what God wants for us! Jesus told us to cut off that which causes us to sin. Matthew 18:8. Since He says our heart is the source of our defilement, His will is for us to surrender our hearts to Him. When we do, He removes the old heart and gives us a new one. Ezekiel 36:26. Then, He will be the faithful Shepherd leading us, His sheep, to green pastures. Psalm 23:1-2.

I won't minimize the difficulty in surrendering the will of our hearts. But if we truly examine the destination of surrender versus the destination of stubbornness, we see that His will is far superior to our will.

2.   Trusting Jesus' concept of righteousness means letting go of our own

A corollary to turning over the will of our hearts to Jesus is trusting His concept of righteousness instead of our own. What happens when someone approaches the King convinced of his own idea of righteousness, rather than seeking the King's righteousness? We see an example in the life of David, the man after God's own heart.

God had anointed David as the next king of Israel while he was still a youth. But he didn't become king immediately. In fact, he spent years on the run from the current king, Saul, who didn't like the idea of David being king. David was 30 years old by the time Saul killed himself after being severely wounded in battle. 1 Samuel 31:3-4.

Some might expect David to celebrate Saul's death under the circumstances. There was at least one guy, an Amalekite, who took that viewpoint. He thought it would be a great thing to bring David the crown of Saul. That seems reasonable, right? After all, David had been anointed the next king of Israel. But this guy took it a step further by (falsely) telling David that he had been the one to kill a mortally wounded Saul, at Saul's own request. 2 Samuel 1:6-10.

The Amalekite apparently thought David would embrace the man who killed Saul. But the Amalekite's idea of righteousness wasn't David's idea of righteousness. David didn't celebrate Saul's death, he mourned it. During those years on the run, David twice had the opportunity to kill Saul, yet would not strike down the Lord's anointed even when his men encouraged him to do so. 1 Samuel 24, 26. David knew he would be king, but trusted the Lord to bring it to pass in His time.

The Amalekite sought the anointed king based on his own idea of righteousness, and it turned out poorly for him. David executed him, saying, "Your blood is on your own head, for your own mouth has testified against you, saying, "I have killed the Lord's anointed."" 2 Samuel 1:14-16. If the Amalekite had sought David's concept of righteousness, he might have still brought David the crown, but he wouldn't have bragged about killing Saul. He would have joined David in mourning over the way his kingship came to pass. That's where David's heart was.

We must not make the same mistake as the Amalekite. When we seek the King, we must leave behind our idea of righteousness and submit to His. If we love Him, we'll love what He loves and hate what He hates. A lot of people say they've given their love to Jesus, yet continue the lifestyle they've always lived. The sad part is, many probably do believe they love Jesus. But they're defining "love" the way our culture defines love, not the way God defines love.

Jesus told us what He meant by "love." He said, "If you love Me, keep My commandments." John 14:15. To make sure we got it, Jesus expanded on this point just a few verses later: "If anyone loves Me, he will keep My word . . . He who does not love Me does not keep My words." John 14:23. So, to Jesus, true love reveals itself through obedience to His word. False love reveals itself through disobedience to His word. If that sounds strange, it might help to look at a fuller definition of the Greek word *agapaó*, translated as "love." It can be defined as "embracing God's will (choosing His choices) and obeying them through His power."[14] If we plug this fuller meaning into John 14:23, it may be easier to grasp Jesus' words: "If anyone [embraces God's will], he will keep My word . . . He who does not [embrace God's will] does not keep My words."

Don't get me wrong—Jesus wasn't saying we earn our salvation through our good deeds. That thinking leads us into the trap of self-righteousness—the idea that we can earn peace with God based on our own goodness. Paul warned about that in explaining how Judaism deviated from saving faith in God. In praying for the salvation of his Jewish people, Paul said, "I bear them witness that they have a zeal for God, but not according to knowledge. For they being ignorant of God's righteousness, and seeking to establish their own righteousness, have not submitted to the righteousness of God." Romans 10:3.

In other words, by trusting in their own righteousness, they failed to seek God's righteousness. This is a faith problem. As Paul explains a few verses earlier, while Israel pursued the law of righteousness, they did not attain it "because they pursued it not by faith but (as if it were possible) by works." Romans 9:32 (NET). We don't want to fall into that same trap.

---

[14] HELPS Word-studies, Helps Ministries, Inc. (1987, 2011) (available at http://biblehub.com/greek/25.htm).

So, if Jesus wasn't saying we need to earn our salvation when He said, "If anyone loves Me, he will keep My word," what was He saying? He was saying that the new root we receive when we accept Him will produce a good fruit of obedience. In contrast, if someone finds that the fruit of his life is disobedience to God's word (for example, porn addiction, sexual immorality, greediness, drunkenness, jealousy, etc.), consider Paul's advice to "examine yourselves, to see whether you are in the faith." 2 Corinthians 13:5 (ESV). That might be uncomfortable, but how much better to recognize the truth while there's still time to find the Truth?

While defining love as "embracing God's will" may not sound like the intimate relationship we desire to have with Jesus, don't lose heart. Jesus wants us to have intimate relationship with Him, as well. In Matthew 10, Jesus said, "He who loves father or mother more than Me is not worthy of Me." Matthew 10:37. Here, we have another Greek word translated "love," but it's not *agapaó*. It's *phileó*. This word can be defined as "to show warm affection in intimate friendship, characterized by tender, heartfelt consideration and kinship."[15]

Both concepts of love need to be part of our relationship with Jesus. We must embrace God's will, yet should also have warm affection in intimate friendship with Him. Think of it like a marriage. The Bible calls wives to obey their husbands—and for husbands to love their wives like Christ loves the church! When a wife has intimate affection for her husband, that obedience becomes less an obligation and more a natural response. How much more true of the church, whose Bridegroom is the King of kings who laid down His life for her! He is so loving and kind that He attracts obedience from His bride!

---

[15] HELPS Word-studies, Helps Ministries, Inc. (1987, 2011) (available at http://biblehub.com/greek/5368.htm).

Jesus' idea of love and righteousness may seem radical to today's Western culture, but it was just as radical in Roman culture. I imagine the Christians in that day faced similar societal pressure that we're seeing in our culture today. That's why Paul wrote in Ephesians, "You may be sure of this, that everyone who is sexually immoral or impure, or who is covetous (that is, an idolater), has no inheritance in the kingdom of God." Ephesians 5:4. Similarly, in 1 Corinthians, in warning that those who practice unrighteousness will not inherit the Kingdom of God, Paul cautioned, "Do not be deceived." 1 Corinthians 6:9-10. Paul was well aware that people would come along and say that you can love Jesus while continuing a practice of sin. But the Bible says you can't. In the words of the apostle John, "No one born of God makes a practice of sinning, for God's seed abides in him, and he cannot keep on sinning because he has been born of God." 1 John 3:9 (ESV).

Don't think that John's claim that no one born of God makes a practice of sinning is unattainable. It's not. As John himself later saw, an innumerable multitude from every tribe, tongue, nation, and people meet this description. Revelation 7:9. So what does John mean by the "practice" of sin? Think about this: we say that doctors "practice" medicine. They should be exercising their discipline regularly to maintain, and even grow, the fruits of their training. John's saying something similar. Are we practicing sin—are we regularly exercising sin, maintaining, or even growing, the fruits of *the* sin? Or are we practicing righteousness—maintaining and growing the fruit of our new root?

If that still sounds tough, remember that John's expectation applies only to those who are born again—those who already have the Spirit of God dwelling inside them. John isn't saying we have to be righteous before seeking God's Kingdom and His righteousness. It's the opposite. Jesus said, "I did not come to call the righteous, but sinners, to repentance." Mark 2:17. If we come to Him, He'll do the cleaning up. That's why Paul, after describing that long list of sinful practices that prevent entry to the Kingdom of God, said, "And such were some of you. But you were washed, but you were sanctified, but you were justified in the name of the Lord Jesus and by the Spirit of our God." 1 Corinthians 6:11. Hallelujah!

So we see that it is God who sanctifies us, not our own efforts. As John put it, "No one born of God makes a practice of sinning, *for* God's seed abides in him, and he cannot keep on sinning because he has been born of God." 1 John 3:9. God's seed doesn't enter us once we overcome the practice of sin. We (that is, those who are born of God) avoid the practice of sin only because God's seed lives in us.

So, rest assured, you don't have to rely on your own righteousness. That's why we seek after His righteousness. Notice where Jesus said He was calling sinners—to repentance. If we're going to seek after His righteousness, we have to repent of our own idea of righteousness. It has to be His righteousness we seek. Only then will we be able to love Jesus the way He defines love.

I know that might have seemed like a tough talk on seeking God's righteousness. So let me wrap this section up with a more personal illustration; not personal to me, but personal to Jesus.

Let's say that you're an 18-year-old girl living in a vast kingdom. Someone shares some news with you: the king's son is romantically interested in you. That's important news! But you want to know more. Who is the king's son? Sure, you know his name—he's famous. But who is he really? What's he like?

What if you kept asking that question to the people who

174

knew him, and all they said was, "He's the king's son! He's the king's son!" Would you eventually get frustrated and yell, "I get it!" Would you maybe say, "To be honest, that's what initially interested me. But now I want to know more about him!"?

I hope you would want to know more about him. Just like I hope you want to know more about who Jesus is. If all you know about Jesus is His position, might that encourage you to love Him for what He has? Would that be true love? But what if you hear about His personality? His righteousness— what He loves and what He hates? Are you more likely to fall in love with who He is? You are with this King, because His personality is amazing! Seek His righteousness!

C. Seeking His Kingdom Requires Us to Count the Cost

I hope that seeking the Kingdom sounds like a good idea to you—it is. But Jesus warned us not to do it lightly. He said, "If anyone wants to be my disciple, you must hate everyone else by comparison[16]—your father and mother, wife and children, brothers and sisters—yes, even your own life. Otherwise, you cannot be My disciple." Luke 14:26 (NLT). In order to leave one kingdom for another, we must love the new Kingdom and fall out of love with the other. Jesus followed this by asking, "Which of you, intending to build a tower, does not sit down first and count the cost, whether he has enough to finish it?" Luke 14:28-29. So Jesus tells us to count the cost of being a disciple, the cost of seeking His Kingdom.

We'll take a high-level look at some things we have to forsake in following Jesus, but let me stress that the King will make you forget the cost. It's a terrible understatement to say He's worth the cost of following Him. If a poor young woman was engaged to a wealthy, loving king, would she care if she had to forsake the $50 in her bank account because her currency wasn't recognized in his kingdom? No—giving up her $50 would be nothing in light of the incredible opportunity!

That said, to someone who is still counting the cost, it doesn't always seem so clear. It's sad to see, but for a drug-addicted prostitute, the cost of forsaking drugs often seems too high a price to pay to find freedom from slavery to a cruel pimp. She just can't see past the addiction. For the man that has everything, the cost of forsaking all to the control of the King of kings is too much. He cannot see past his limited

---

[16] That is, our love for Jesus should so outshine our love for everyone else that even our love for our family seems like hate in comparison to our love for Jesus.

abilities. Unbelievers can similarly view the cost of following Jesus as simply too high, and Satan tries to keep it that way by blinding unbelievers to the glory of Christ. 2 Corinthians 4:4-5.

Satan's active effort to blind the unbelieving makes it all the more important that believers engage in the ongoing battle against the spiritual enemies of Christ. Ephesians 6:10-20. Those who have already counted the cost—and discovered that "everything else is worthless when compared with the infinite value of knowing Christ"—shine like a lamp on a stand. Philippians 3:8 (NLT); Matthew 5:15. God "has shone in our hearts to give the light of the knowledge of the glory of God in the face of Jesus Christ." 2 Corinthians 4:6.

With that in mind, let's look at some of those costs that turn out to be not so costly when we discover the infinite, inherent value of Christ.

1.   The cost of throwing open the gates to your heart

One of the costs of seeking God's Kingdom is our title. Even though everyone without Christ is under Satan's jurisdiction, people usually think of themselves as the king of their own kingdom. And Satan plays into that because he knows that people (in an unredeemed condition) crave control and don't want to give it up. So, even though Satan is the ruler of this world, he is willing to let someone use the title "king." As in, "I'm the king of my life." But that's all it will be—an inflated title.

Satan tried to lure Jesus with this inflated title. When Satan tested Jesus in the wilderness, he "showed Him all the kingdoms of the world and all their glory. And he said to Him, 'All these things I will give You if You will fall down and worship me.'" Matthew 4:8-9. In other words, Satan said, "I'll let you call yourself king, but your actions will demonstrate who the real king is." Jesus wasn't having any of it, responding, "Away with you, Satan! For it is written, 'You shall worship the LORD your God, and Him only you shall serve." Matthew 4:10.

If Satan's best offer to Jesus, the Son of God, still required Jesus to worship Satan in exchange for the illusion of power, why do we think we will be any different? If we're buying into the idea that we are the king of our life, will we throw open the gates to our heart—our kingdom—and welcome in the King? Probably not. So we have to lose the title.

Jesus made essentially this very point in a parable. He asked, "What king, going to make war against another king, does not sit down first and consider whether he is able with ten thousand to meet him who comes against him with twenty thousand?" Luke 14:31. Think about it. Until we surrender to Christ, the King of kings, we are all in the position of that king going to war against a stronger King. If someone sits down and thinks about it, like a rational king would do, he will realize he has no hope of defeating King Jesus.

Jesus went on, describing what a rational king does when he realizes he cannot defeat the stronger king: "While the other is still a great way off, he sends a delegation and asks conditions of peace." Luke 14:33. In other words, the rational king, realizing that peace is his only chance, asks how he can reconcile himself to the stronger king. There is no army large enough to make war with the King of kings, so we are well advised to choose peace on His terms. Job 22:21-28. That's what God wants us to do. While He will march into battle against those who oppose Him, He wants all those little kings to do the opposite, calling them to come "trembling out of their fortresses." Psalm 18:45. He says, "Let them lay hold of my protection, let them make peace with me." Isaiah 27:4-5.

What terms of peace does the King offer? Total surrender. Jesus concluded the parable by saying, "So likewise, whoever of you does not forsake all that he has cannot be My disciple." Luke 14:33. The Kingdom of God is marching toward our kingdom, and it is not stopping. Jesus' delay in arriving is neither weakness nor forgetfulness; it is His patience and kindness, which is meant to lead to repentance. Romans 2:4. He does not wish "that any should perish, but that all should reach repentance." 2 Peter 3:9.

In other words, God wants people to realize they cannot defeat the King; they must surrender and accept His terms of peace. Like Isaiah said, "Seek the Lord while He may be found." Isaiah 55:6. For those who don't throw open the gates of their kingdom and welcome the King, the King will come nonetheless. Like He said to Israel in their days of rebellion, "Prepare to meet your God." Amos 4:12. And at that point, it will be too late—He will strike down the kings who set themselves against Him. Revelation 21:11-16; Psalm 2:1-12.

That may sound tough. But it's not so tough if we start loving Jesus for who He is, rather than just for what He does—if we start looking at the world as His kingdom rather than ours. When we love Him for who He is, we can love what He loves—and hate what He hates. We will be able to say, "Seven times a day I praise you, because of Your righteous judgments." Psalm 119:64. Truly, "the judgments of the Lord are . . . sweeter also than honey and the honeycomb." Psalm 19:9-10.

When we really understand that God is love, it's not so hard to count the cost of seeking His Kingdom and willingly forsaking everything. When we begin to understand "the width and length and depth and height" of Christ's love, we understand why the Song of Solomon says that even "if a man were to give all the riches of his house for love, it would be utterly despised." Song of Solomon 8:7 (NASB).

But if our riches are despised, what can we give to the God who said, "Whatever is under the whole heaven is mine"? Job 41:11. Let us offer the only thing we can: Let us, by the mercies of God, offer our "bodies as a living sacrifice, holy and pleasing to God." Romans 12:1 (NIV). This is "true and proper worship"—the only reasonable response to Him. Romans 12:1 (NIV). He wants us to give the one thing we have to give Him—ourselves. The King wants us to sacrifice our kingdoms to receive His Kingdom. When we give Him what He desires, we will declare His name not our own. "Let us continually offer to God a sacrifice of praise—the fruit of lips that openly profess his name!" Hebrews 13:15 (NIV).

Not only that, but when we recognize Jesus' rightful place as King, it allows Him to give us the benefits of His Kingdom. He has amazing things for those who count the cost and seek His Kingdom. We'll talk about those in a little bit. But we only get there after throwing open our hearts to Him.

2.   Jonathan shows what it means to forsake our personal kingdom

What does it look like to surrender your kingdom to the rightful king? Let me tell you about a man named Jonathan. Jonathan was a prince of Israel, the son of Saul, the first king of Israel. Jonathan was slated to be the second king of Israel. But God had a different plan.

After King Saul rejected God's commands, the Lord rejected Saul from being king over Israel. Samuel the prophet told Saul, "The LORD has torn the kingdom of Israel from you this day and has given it to a neighbor of yours, who is better than you." 1 Samuel 15:28 (ESV). God sent Samuel to anoint a youth named David to be the next king of Israel.

You've heard of David—he's the one who killed the giant, Goliath.

After David killed Goliath, Saul gave David a high position in the military, and David's success grew. It grew so much that women began singing, "Saul has struck down his thousands, and David his ten thousands." 1 Samuel 18:7 (ESV). This sparked Saul's jealousy. He thought, "What more can he have but the kingdom?" 1 Samuel 18:8 (ESV).

Soon, Saul began efforts to kill David to preserve his place on the throne of his kingdom. These efforts continued on and off until Saul's death years later. So rather than voluntarily cede his kingdom to the Lord's anointed, Saul fought to hang onto his kingdom till the bitter end.

Jonathan took a different course of action. From the time David killed Goliath, "Jonathan made a covenant with David, because he loved him as his own soul." 1 Samuel 18:3 (ESV). Jonathan "stripped himself of the robe that was on him and gave it to David," not to mention his armor and weapons. 1 Samuel 18:4 (ESV). Jonathan even interceded with his jealous father on David's behalf and, when Saul's murderous intentions became clear, assisted David in fleeing Saul's royal stronghold.

This cost Jonathan. First, it cost him with his father. Saul realized that Jonathan was helping David and publicly disgraced him. Saul said, "You son of a perverse, rebellious woman, do I not know that you have chosen the son of Jesse to your own shame, and to the shame of your mother's nakedness?" 1 Samuel 20:30 (ESV). Those words hurt, but Saul had a reason for his anger. He put all the cards on the table next: "For as long as the son of Jesse lives on the earth, neither you nor your kingdom shall be established." 1 Samuel 18:31 (ESV).

This was a second cost to Jonathan in making a covenant with David. If David would be the next king of Israel, it meant that Jonathan would not be the next king of Israel. Jonathan's choice involved more than simply giving up his opportunity to be king. When one dynasty gives way to a new dynasty, it doesn't usually end well for the remaining members of the old dynasty. Don't think Jonathan hadn't considered this risk; he asked David to spare him and his family when David's kingdom came. 1 Samuel 18:15.

Yet, even though it would require Jonathan to forsake his kingship and possibly even his life, "Jonathan made a covenant with the house of David, saying . . . 'The Lord shall be between me and you, and between my offspring and your offspring, forever.'" 1 Samuel 20:16, 42 (ESV). As part of this covenant, Jonathan prayed, "May the Lord take vengeance on David's enemies." 1 Samuel 20:16 (ESV). Those aren't light words considering that his father, his king, was David's enemy.

Jonathan made a choice. He chose David, the anointed king, over his own kingship. And he stuck by that choice faithfully, even when David remained on the run from Saul for years. Jonathan even compounded his treason against his father by giving aid and comfort to David, going to him in his wilderness hideout, where he "strengthened his hand in God." 1 Samuel 23:16 (ESV). In the midst of this season of testing for David, Jonathan remained firm, saying, "You shall be king over Israel, and I shall be next to you." 1 Samuel 23:17.

Jonathan's desire has been partially fulfilled—David became king over Israel. But it has not seen complete fulfillment, as Jonathan died in battle against the Philistines, leading his mortally wounded father to commit suicide. 1 Samuel 31:2-4. But like the book of Hebrews tells of those faithful men and women who looked forward to a heavenly country rather than an earthly one, I wouldn't be surprised to one day see Jonathan standing next to David in an eternal Kingdom. Let us forsake the path of Saul and choose the path of Jonathan! Let us forsake our earthly kingdom so we may stand next to the King of kings!

3. Exchanging worldly wisdom for Godly wisdom

a) Letting go of the fear of having nothing

Another cost of seeking His Kingdom is letting go of worldly wisdom. Why is the world's wisdom so bad? To start with, worldly wisdom is not wisdom at all because it lacks the beginning of wisdom—the fear of the Lord. Proverbs 9:10. Worldly wisdom replaces God's counsel with man's (individual or collective). Worldly wisdom is man's conversation instead of Heavenly conversation.

If we're going to seek God's Kingdom, we must be willing to stop listening to the world's logic and reasoning, and to begin listening to an authority higher than our worldly wisdom—God. That means we can't "conform to the pattern of this world" (Rom. 12:2 (NIV)), because the world follows Satan's culture. Satan's culture isn't limited to extravagant sins like murder, stealing, adultery, etc. Satan's culture is simply living for one's personal kingdom instead of God's. When we're living for our personal kingdom, we focus on things like self-glorification, wealth, preservation, comfort, and security. When focused on our kingdoms, we listen to counsel that justifies our focus on ourselves. That's what Paul's talking about when he says we can't conform to the pattern of the world. Instead, Paul says, "be transformed by the renewing of your mind. Then you will be able to test and approve what God's will is—his good, pleasing and perfect will." Romans 12:2 (NIV).

We could look at many examples showing how easy it is to

follow worldly wisdom instead of Godly wisdom, but we'll pick just one. Previously, we looked at Jonathan's life as an example of how to surrender our personal thrones to the King. Now, let's focus on his father, Saul. Saul was chosen by God to be the first king of Israel. 1 Samuel 10:24. King Saul began his journey humbly and feared God, not men. 1 Samuel 10:26 -11:13. But as time passed, Saul began to exchange the wisdom of God for the wisdom of men because he began desiring the praises of men. His desire for the praise of men grew so intense that it came to a point where he became jealous of a shepherd boy (David) who had such military success that the entire nation began praising his feats, saying, "Saul has slain his thousands, and David his ten thousands." 1 Samuel 18:7. Saul was the king of Israel, but he feared David would take his throne away from him. 1 Samuel 18:8-9.

According to worldly wisdom, Saul's fear was probably justified. World history offers many stories of kings losing their thrones to strong, popular men rising within their kingdoms. But what did this worldly wisdom produce in Saul? His desire to maintain his kingdom was driving him to the point of insanity. His fear of man's response (or lack thereof) to his leadership was outweighing the fear of God. He seems to have forgotten that God anointed him as king of Israel, not the people. The duration of Saul's kingdom depended not on man's opinion, but upon God's sovereign decree. Daniel 4:17.

We see Saul's misplaced fear of man over God demonstrated through his choice of whose voice to obey in 1 Samuel 15. God instructed Saul to completely destroy the sinful kingdom of the Amalekites, fulfilling God's promise to destroy the Amalekites after they attacked Israel as God led them out of Egypt: "Now go and attack Amalek and utterly destroy all that they have, and do not spare them. But kill both man and woman, infant and nursing child, ox and sheep, camel and donkey." 1 Samuel 15:3; Exodus 17:14. While Saul did conquer Amalek, he did not fully obey God by destroying all. 1 Samuel 15:17-24. Saul and his men were unwilling to destroy the best of the livestock, so he allowed his men to keep them, ostensibly for the purpose of sacrificing them to God. They also kept alive the king of the Amalekites, contrary to God's instruction.

Scripture tells us that when Saul was confronted by Samuel, the prophet of God, regarding his disobedience, he explained that he transgressed God's command because he feared the people. 1 Samuel 15:24. Because Saul was focused on self-preservation and glory, he lusted for the praise of men. This led him to turn his ear to earthly wisdom. As a leader, it would seem wise to pay a reward to your warriors who had just risked their lives to fight your battle. That makes even more sense given that the Israelite warriors supposedly intended to sacrifice that reward to the very God who had ordered them into battle. According to worldly wisdom, Saul's decision was logical. But Saul wasn't anointed king by man, and man (or man's wisdom) wasn't supposed to be his ultimate authority. Saul's wrong heart deafened him to Godly wisdom, leaving him with ears only for worldly wisdom. This worldly wisdom led him to focus on his personal kingdom instead of God's Kingdom. Saul's desire for self-preservation and glory caused him to pursue the praise of men instead of God. Worldly wisdom pleases men, while heavenly wisdom pleases God. Both types of wisdom begin with fear, but one begins with a fear that leads to peace with God, while the other is focused on achieving peace with men.

Sometimes it is easy to judge someone like Saul and believe that we are nothing like him. Could this be because our nature is to protect our kingdom, believing we are a better version of ourselves than the evidence proves? Most of us want to believe we are more like David, "a man after God's own heart." I hope you are more like David then Saul!

But let's not assume Saul's story has no application to us without further consideration. It would be heavenly wisdom to ask the Holy Spirit to search the intention of our hearts.

Today in America, conventional wisdom tells us to plan carefully for our retirement. Because this idea seems to be common sense, there are literally entire industries focused solely on helping people store up more treasure to (hopefully) have enough money to last through retirement years. The fear of not having enough fuels this huge industry.

This idea of trying to conquer the fear of not having enough by obtaining more makes sense from a worldly perspective—who likes the idea of living out their last years with no resources? Having money in retirement is not a problem. But allowing the fear of not having enough to drive your decision-making is a problem. This fear shares the same root as the fear that consumed King Saul. Saul was motivated by self-preservation, just like so many of us today. Do you think the result will be different for us if we aren't delivered from this fear of not having enough?

The fear of not having enough impacts people's decision-making. For example, it causes many to hold back in their giving. This is the opposite of the early church in the book of Acts. The early church was extravagant in giving! People sold their fields—their investments for the future—to make sure all were provided for. That is freely giving. They gave to the point that no one in the church was in need. What! No one in need!

In contrast to the early church, when someone is focused on his own kingdom's security, rather than God's Kingdom, he stores up earthly treasures. This is acting according to the wisdom of men. Jesus, the King of kings, tells us to think differently. He says, "Do not lay up for yourselves treasures on earth, where moth and rust destroy and where thieves break in and steal; but lay up for yourselves treasures in heaven." Matthew 6:19-20. Jesus followed this with a very practical reason for this instruction: "For where your treasure is, there your heart will be also." Matthew 6:21. We want our hearts to be focused on heaven, not earth.

Fear of not having enough will cause someone to focus on earthly treasures. It does not mean that someone in bondage to fear will not give. But he will tend to give out of his abundance, rather than sacrificially, as the Lord may ask. According to the wisdom of the world, this is both good and wise. But like Saul, he will be only partially obedient to God's call. His obedience will be limited by the worldly wisdom of self-preservation. Someone can give big checks while still living under the fear of self-preservation. He has enough to give. It is when someone gives everything he has, like the poor widow who gave all she had—two small coins—that he demonstrates true freedom from self-absorption. That is Kingdom culture.

When someone invests not in their temporal future, but in the Kingdom of God, you know he is free from the bondage of Saul and more like David. He is not focused on his own kingdom, but is in love with the Kingdom of God. If you're subject to the fear of having nothing (or just not as much as you want), then you cannot give freely. Therefore, you cannot obey God fully. Giving freely is a willingness to give all, no matter what, who, or how it will affect. It is having the grace of God empowering you to ignore the fleshly instinct toward self-preservation. With this grace on your life, you experience freedom from the world's culture of loving what man loves and hating what man hates (including not having enough). You no longer love self-preservation, but the increase of the Kingdom of God. People with this freedom can be amazing stewards because they are emotionally, mentally, and spiritually in His presence, free from the worries and fears of tomorrow. That person is free from the fear not having enough because he has all, King Jesus!

b)   Exchanging our name for His name

Worldly wisdom does not just counsel us to take care of ourselves, it declares that we are wise to make a name for ourselves. Having a name in the world is the ultimate success. Many people want their name to be known around the world. Fame brings wealth, influence, and power in this age. To have your name known by all is the ultimate glory. And, in that sense, today isn't much different than days past.

The world's love of fame should give us pause. Think back to Genesis. Why did God confuse the language of mankind (that is, create multiple languages so people no longer spoke one language) at the tower of Babel? Because the people said, "Let us build for ourselves a city, and a tower whose top is in the heavens." They said, "Let us make a name for ourselves." Genesis 11:4. They didn't want to praise the name of God; they wanted to make a name for themselves. They didn't want God's Kingdom to come to earth; they wanted to take their kingdom to heaven.

James says that such focus on selfish ambitious is earthly and unspiritual. But it's more than that—he says it is demonic. What does that mean? It means that worldly wisdom—selfish ambition—comes from demons.

That may sound a little crazy to our ears, steeped in Western culture. Most of us were raised in public schools and universities that long ago adopted a worldview that left no room for God, much less for demons. We have been conditioned to give no heed to the spiritual world. But ignoring it doesn't make it less real. If you struggle to attribute worldly wisdom to demons, think back to what provoked Lucifer's fall. His "I wills." He succumbed to selfish ambition, and has never stopped spreading his "wisdom" in the world.

I'm telling you to let go of worldly wisdom, but I don't want to leave you with a vacuum. If I'm saying we should remove worldly wisdom from its pedestal, what do we replace it with? Let's look at what God recommends: "Let not the wise man glory in his wisdom . . . but let him who glories glory in this, that he understands and knows Me, that I am the LORD, exercising lovingkindness, justice, and righteousness in the earth." Jeremiah 9:23-24 (MEV). God wants us to care more about knowing who He is than about knowing worldly wisdom. Why does God want us to know His ways (lovingkindness, justice, and righteousness—more than worldly wisdom)? Because, He says, "in these things I delight." Jeremiah 9:24 (MEV).

We also don't need to make a name for ourselves. God, the Creator of the heavens and earth, loves to give us His name. A young woman in love dreams of carrying the name of her betrothed. We, the bride of Christ, should share that young bride's glory in being called by the name of her husband. May King Jesus delight in us because we are known by His name. May we love bearing His name so His life is our delight. He wants us to love what He loves and hate what He hates.

Letting go of worldly wisdom takes endurance. But it's no different for us than it was in Paul's day. Truly, "there is nothing new under the sun" (Ecc. 1:9), and "no temptation has overtaken [us] except such as is common to man." 1 Cor. 10:13.

4.   The cost of following Jesus includes our unforgiveness

When we talk about the cost of surrendering our kingdom, most of us probably first think about the desires of the flesh, inappropriate relationships, or material possessions. While that's true, it's more than that. We have to surrender everything, including the bitterness of unforgiveness.

You might be asking, "Why would anyone want to hang on to their bitterness?" Good question, but sometimes we grip more tightly to our bitterness than we do our wealth. The author of Hebrews understood the seductiveness of bitterness, and warned against it: "See to it that no one fails to obtain the grace of God; that no 'root of bitterness' springs up and causes trouble, and by it many become defiled." Hebrews 12:15 (ESV). He even goes on to suggest that a root of bitterness gives rise to sexual immorality and unholiness. Hebrews 12:16.

Why would bitterness lead to sexual immorality and unholiness? People struggle with bitterness because they are hurt. Hurt people often make bad decisions, looking for love in all the wrong places. Bad company ruins good morals. 1 Corinthians 15:33. That path leads us away from the grace of God.

Many of us probably don't think of our unforgiveness as a symptom that we're still sitting on the throne of our heart. But it is. Unforgiveness usually exists because someone has harmed us. We have a grievance against another person. Another king has damaged our kingdom—we've been victimized by another king in his quest to advance his or her personal kingdom. This is nothing new. If we look through the histories of the Old Testament kingdoms, I think we'll find that every kingdom was victimized by another king at some point—some very badly.

The question is, what happens to those old grievances when we open the gates of our heart to Jesus? Many of us want to hang on to our grievances until we make sure the wrongs are righted—or maybe even after the wrongs have been righted. But that's not how it works.

When one king turns the kingdom over to another, he loses the right to say, "Vengeance is mine!" It's now up to the new king to deal with the situation as he sees fit. This is true with our personal kingdoms, as well. If we're going to welcome Jesus onto the throne of our hearts, we have to give Him all the records—including the list of outstanding grievances. We can't say, "Jesus, you're my King. But, I'm sure You'll understand that I'm going to keep fighting these old battles as I see fit." We have to say, "No longer will I fight my battles, the battle is the Lord's." See 1 Samuel 17:47. We have to put down our swords and say, "O Lord of hosts, who judges righteously . . . to You have I committed my cause." Jeremiah 11:20. Because He is the one entitled to say, "Vengeance is Mine." Romans 12:19.

For those of us who struggle with forgiveness, the disciples were right there with us. Peter heard Jesus say near the start of His ministry, "If you forgive others their trespasses, your heavenly Father will also forgive you, but if you do not forgive others their trespasses, neither will your Father forgive your trespasses." Matthew 6:14-15. Yet Peter came to Jesus later in His ministry, asking how many times he should forgive his brother. Peter apparently thought seven times was surely enough to justify holding a grudge. Matthew 18:21.

Jesus disagreed, telling a parable illustrating that we should focus on God's forgiveness of our sins rather than the sins of others against us. In the parable, a king wanted to settle up with his servants who owed him money. One of them owed him 10,000 talents. Matthew 18:24. That was a huge amount of money, since each talent represented 20 years of wages for a laborer. That would be hundreds of millions or even billions of dollars in today's money. But when the servant couldn't pay, the king "was moved with compassion, released him, and forgave him the debt." Matthew 18:27.

You would think that, having been forgiven such an enormous amount of money, the servant would be in a generous mood. But no, when he came across a fellow servant who owed him 100 days' wages, he started choking the guy and threw him in prison. Matthew 18:28-20. When the king heard about it, he said, "You wicked servant! I forgave you all that debt because you begged me. Should you not also have had compassion on your fellow servant, just as I had on you?" Matthew 18:32-33. The king "delivered him to the torturers until he should pay all that was due him." Matthew 18:34. I imagine the disciples looking around at each other uncomfortably as Jesus ends the parable, and then he added the icing on the cake: "So My heavenly Father also will do to you if each of you, from his heart, does not forgive his brother his trespasses." Matthew 18:35.

I'm not saying this makes sense from a worldly perspective. Nor am I saying it is easy. Some of us have been brutally wronged, suffering even severe physical and sexual abuse at the hands of those who were supposed to love and protect us. But Jesus didn't say it was easy. Jesus just said it was necessary.

In the parable, the wicked servant had a legitimate claim against his fellow servant. The guy owed him 100 days' wages. That was a lot of money. But it paled in comparison to the amount the wicked servant owed the king—only 1/10,000 of a percent. What was Jesus trying to tell us about the magnitude of His forgiveness toward us?

We need to ponder what Jesus is forgiving versus what we are forgiving. When someone harms another person, he is seeking to advance his personal kingdom, even at the expense of another person's kingdom. When our kingdom is the victim of an attack, we often want God to execute justice and make things right before we will forgive. But God has a different culture. He asks us to forgive the attacking kingdom even if we do not see immediate justice.

Why does God command us to forgive a king who attacks our kingdom? If we've surrendered our kingdom to God, then we no longer have a kingdom to be attacked. God will execute justice according to His will. Either the guilty kingdom will be judged for its deeds, or that false king will surrender his kingdom to God, with Jesus taking the punishment for his sins, just as He did ours. Either way, God will execute justice in His kingdom. We can trust His leadership.

But if we still have a kingdom to be attacked, it means we're still guilty of a greater crime against God. No matter what bad deed some other king committed against our kingdom, we're committing a greater crime. How do I know? Worse than a king invading another kingdom is a servant or son who takes the throne from the King—that's treason. Treason is the ultimate violation of justice. Treason arises from within the heart of the kingdom, whereas an attack by another kingdom comes from the outside.

All the other false kings are in the same position—all are guilty of treason against the true King. This is a bigger problem for each false king than whatever war crimes he commits against other personal kingdoms. So even though we may squabble with other kings, we put those differences aside to join together in a conspiracy to hold onto our stolen thrones by conspiring to kill the true King (praise God, the King of kings cannot be conquered by death!). Therefore, while we may have a legitimate complaint against another king, it pales in comparison to our own treason against the King of kings.

Despite this truth, a false king will often blame the King of kings for not protecting his personal kingdom from attack. These "kings" tend to be angry at God because they do not experience "justice" on their terms. But since our personal kingdoms arise from the worst injustice (treason against the true King), our thrones were never actually ours. So, then, what entitles us to tell the King of kings what justice is?

Imagine the magnitude of forgiveness the King of kings has toward us who did not just commit treason, but then blamed him for everything that has gone wrong in our kingdoms. So if He will forgive us for such intense violation and pain, what response can we have toward others who have hurt us—even those unrepentant kings still trying to hold on to their thrones? Those who have surrendered their kingdoms to God and received forgiveness for treason have no right to withhold forgiveness to other false kings for lesser crimes.

Now think about the price Jesus paid so we could be forgiven of our treasons. Think about the One who paid the price. Isaiah heard the angels in heaven singing these words about Jesus: "Holy, holy, holy is the Lord of hosts; the whole earth is full of His glory!" Isaiah 6:4. Yet, while we were still sinners, this One who knew no sin became sin for us. Romans 5:8; 2 Corinthians 5:21. It is "through His blood [that we have] the forgiveness of sin." Ephesians 1:7. This is the price that He paid for us. 1 Corinthians 6:20.

I understand that it will cost some of us a lot to forgive. And for some of us, it's not just about forgiving others, but also ourselves. But whatever the cost, it pales in comparison to the price He paid that we might be forgiven. While we might not have the strength to forgive on our own, that's why we seek His righteousness. He says, "My grace is sufficient for you, for My strength is made perfect in weakness." 2 Corinthians 12:9.

Unforgiveness makes people weary. Jesus says, "Come to

Me, all who are weary and heavy-laden." Matthew 11:28 (NASB). He says, "Take My yoke upon you and learn from Me." Matthew 11:29 (NASB). What do we learn from Him? Think about what He said as they crucified Him: "Father, forgive them, for they do not know what they are doing." Luke 23:34 (NASB). When we learn His way, He says, "you will find rest for your souls." Matthew 11:29 (NASB).

To you who are weary from unforgiveness: are you ready to come to Him and trade bitterness for rest and walk in salvation? "In returning and rest you will be saved." Isaiah 30:15.

5.   Coming into His kingdom

If we seek first God's Kingdom, we will find it. But the Kingdom is surrounded by a wall—we can't enter by our own will. If our image of heaven is an open sky, this may come as a shock. But don't be fooled into thinking the wall is bad news. Sure, the wall does keep out those who are still at war with the King, but that's no problem if we are willing to accept the King's terms of peace. The wall that keeps out His enemies also protects those who enter His Kingdom.

And for those of us who have left our own kingdoms in search of His, it's a joyful day when we stumble upon that wall after wandering around in the wilderness. You may ask, "Why is the wall cause for joy?" Because we know there is a way in. Remember that Jesus said, "Enter by the narrow gate." Matthew 7:13 (ESV). God wants all to enter! 2 Peter 3:9.

The wall will guide us to the entrance, if only we follow it around. The poor in spirit don't give up when they find the wall; they seek the way in with violent intensity, passionate for the King. Matthew 11:12. They are that desperate to surrender their reign in exchange for His. What do these passionate seekers of His Kingdom find? They find Jesus the Christ. Jesus said, "I am the door." John 10:7. He is that narrow gate!

What do people do when confronted with a locked door? They knock or leave. Jesus says, "Knock, and it will be opened to you." Matthew 7:7. But if we don't have eyes to see the door, how would we know to knock? So who will knock at the door? Only those who recognize Jesus for who He is—the door to the Kingdom. They will cry out, "This is the gate of the LORD, through which the righteous shall enter." Psalm 118:20. They will say, "Open to me the gates of righteousness; I will go through them, and I will praise the LORD. . . . For you have answered me, and have become my salvation!" Psalm 118:19, 21.

The ones who enter are those who submit to the King of the Kingdom, those who aren't hanging onto their crowns for a more opportune moment. The ones who enter are those who give up on *the* sin—the desire to be king. The poor in spirit. The poor in spirit confess that Jesus is Lord—(the King) and believe in their heart that He is who He said He is—He who died, but behold, is alive forevermore because God raised Him from the dead. Romans 10:9; Revelation 1:18. Those who love the King and His culture find "redemption, the forgiveness of sins . . . by the blood of the cross." Colossians 1:13, 20. They are delivered "from the domain of darkness and transferred . . . to the kingdom of His beloved Son." Colossians 1:13. The poor in Spirit "enter into His gates with thanksgiving, and into His courts with praise!" Psalm 100:4.

Once we enter His Kingdom, we can receive the benefits of citizenship. I promised we would get to this, but we had to first understand the need to count the cost, the need to accept the terms of peace—total surrender—that Jesus described in Luke 14.

While the "peace" that comes after surrendering to a human army is often unpleasant (that is, forced occupation), that's not how it works with King Jesus. Once we put our trust in the King, "we have peace with God through our Lord Jesus Christ." Romans 5:1. Jesus said, "Peace I leave with you, My peace I give to you; not as the world gives do I give to you." John 14:27. What's the difference between the world's peace and Jesus' peace? The world's peace is outwardly focused, depending on physical circumstances. Jesus' peace comes from the Holy Spirit, who dwells inside those who accept the King.

Peace with God brings joy, not just an emotional high, but a deep-seated wellness that comes from reconciliation to the God who made us. Those at peace with God "rejoice in hope of the glory of God." Romans 5:2. This peace of God, "which surpasses all understanding, will guard your hearts and minds through Christ Jesus." Philippians 4:7. It's for that reason that Paul was able to say that those who obtain peace through Christ will "glory in tribulations, knowing that tribulation produces perseverance; and perseverance, character; and character, hope." Romans 5:4.

Immediately after Jesus explained the terms of peace in Luke 14, the Holy Spirit prompted Luke to devote the entirety of Luke 15 to Jesus' description of the celebration in heaven over each sinner who repents, that is, everyone who surrenders his or her throne to Christ. This demonstrates just how important each one of us is to God. The mere fact that a bunch of other people have already repented does not lessen the "joy in the presence of the angels of God over one sinner who repents." Luke 15:9.

And it's not just the angels who rejoice—the Father rejoices, as well. In the parable of the prodigal son, Jesus describes a son who blows a fortune on prostitutes and wild living. Luke 15:13, 30. With nothing left, he becomes a starving servant in a foreign land. After a while, "He came to his senses." Luke 15:17 (NASB). He travels back home, prepared to repent and beg his father to take him on as a hired servant. But he only gets a chance to repent.

When his father sees him coming from a great way off, his father "had compassion, and ran and fell on his neck and kissed him." Luke 15:20. You might say, "Wait, isn't that backwards?" Why should the father have gone out to meet the son? Why didn't he make the son come to him and fall at his feet? But that's not how God operates. God hopes that we "might grope for Him and find Him, though He is not far from each one of us." Acts 17:27. What happens when we draw near to God? "He will draw near to you." James 4:8. That's what the story of the prodigal son illustrates.

Not only does God draw near to us, but He makes those who surrender everything to Christ His children. When the prodigal son repented, the father didn't relegate him to the status of a lowly servant. He said, "Bring out the best robe and put it on him, and put a ring on his hand and sandals on his feet. And bring the fatted calf here and kill it, and let us eat and be merry; for this my son was dead and is alive again; he was lost and is found." Luke 15:22-24.

How amazing is that! When we surrender to Christ our illusory kingdom, we don't just become citizens of His Kingdom. We become children of God. And like the father gave the prodigal son the robe and the ring, God's children "shall reign on the earth" in His Kingdom. Revelation 7:10. After we got off His throne, He turns around and invites us to "come boldly unto the throne of grace." Hebrews 4:16 (KJV).

Yes, the benefits of citizenship in Jesus' Kingdom are incredible. One receives a perfect Father, a perfect Friend, authority in His Kingdom, access to the throne room, eternal joy and so much more. I could go on and on about the benefits of living in God's Kingdom, but I'd rather let you seek His Kingdom and discover them yourself.

In fact, while the benefits are great, it's the King Himself who is truly amazing. What kind of King offers that benefit to those who tried to take His throne from Him? The King of kings. The Creator who put on flesh and tabernacled among us. To Him be the glory and dominion forever and ever! 1 Peter 5:11; Romans 11:36.

I think we see a preview of the breathtaking presence of Jesus in the story of King Solomon and the Queen of Sheba. The queen "heard about the fame of Solomon and his relationship to the Lord, [and] she came to test Solomon with hard questions." 1 Kings 10:1 (NIV). But "Solomon answered all her questions; nothing was too hard for the king to explain to her." 1 Kings 10:3 (NIV). When the queen "saw all the wisdom of Solomon and the palace he had built, the food on his table, the seating of his officials, the attending servants in their robes, his cupbearers, and the burnt offerings he made at the temple of the Lord, she was overwhelmed." 1 Kings 10:4-5 (NIV).

Notice that while she was impressed with Solomon's stuff, it began with Solomon himself. See what the queen said, "The report I heard in my own country about your achievements and your wisdom is true. But I did not believe these things until I came and saw with my own eyes. Indeed, not even half was told me; in wisdom and wealth you have far exceeded the report I heard." 1 Kings 10:6-7 (NIV). I think we'll have a similar reaction when we meet the King of kings. We've heard about Him, but He will far exceed the report we've heard!

The queen also recognized how blessed were Solomon's servants who stood in his presence: "How happy your people must be! How happy your officials, who continually stand before you and hear your wisdom!" 1 Kings 10:8 (NIV). How well do these words apply to those who will stand in the presence of King Jesus? As the queen of Sheba recognized, God blessed Israel by placing Solomon on the throne: "Praise be to the Lord your God, who has delighted in you and placed you on the throne of Israel. Because of the Lord's eternal love for Israel, he has made you king to maintain justice and righteousness." 1 Kings 10:8-9 (NIV). How much more did God bless not just Israel, but the nations, by placing Jesus on the throne?

D.   Receiving That Which is of First Importance: The One Who Went to the Cross

As we wrap up this journey together, I want to deliver "to you as of first importance what I also received: that Christ died for our sins in accordance with the Scriptures, that he was buried, [and] that he was raised on the third day in accordance with the Scriptures." 1 Corinthians 15:3-4 (ESV).

Without Christ's work on the cross, we could have no part in the Kingdom of Heaven. He paid the penalty for our treason. When we understand just who He is, we'll appreciate His work of the cross so much more.

1.   Coming to terms with our treason

To understand who He is, we first need to understand who we are. We need to come to terms with the gravity of our treason.

a)   Inciting others to treason

The realization that I am a false king sitting on the throne of the Almighty King should be a very fearful thing. It's even scarier when we recognize that how we live influences those around us. Think of Jesus' words to the Pharisees: "You travel over land and sea to win a single convert, and when you have succeeded, you make them twice as much a child of hell as you are." Matthew 23:15. When we say we can serve the King while sitting on His throne, we lead others to believe they can do the same, leading them further astray from the true King (whether we intend to or not). Not only are we guilty of treason ourselves, but we're guilty of inciting others into treason.

That used to be me. I was so vain, I thought the Gospel was about me. I was a "good" person—a good pastor—who realized later that I had been sitting on a throne that wasn't mine. In my own deception, I believed I could be reconciled to God without surrendering my kingdom and falling in love with what He loves and hating what He hates. I viewed heaven (and my salvation from hell) as the subject of the conversation instead of God. Jesus was merely the object of the conversation—my ticket into Heaven.

Once I realized that Jesus (not to mention John the Baptist and Paul) preached the Gospel of the *Kingdom*, I saw the error of my ways. The Gospel doesn't allow me to go to heaven (that is, to live with the King) while remaining the king of my life. It couldn't. Because the Gospel, the Good News, is that He is the King of kings and has come with His dominion/culture so that those who are poor in spirit, done with *the* sin—can be delivered into *His* Kingdom through His work on the cross. There's no room for my kingship in His kingdom.

But I hadn't just been deceived—I was also a deceiver. Since I was a sincere believer in this partial gospel, I led many other people to believe the same thing. Sure, I told them to repent of the sinful things they did, but I didn't tell them to repent of *the* sin. I was like the priests in Jeremiah's day, who said to the people, "'Peace, peace!' when there is no peace."

Jeremiah 29:11. I led them to believe their treason was acceptable, that they could be reconciled to God without surrendering their kingdom.

I have the honor of being on staff at the Atlanta Dream Center Church. We're passionate about seeing the lost reached, rescued, and restored to Christ. When I say passion, I don't say it lightly. In 2015, we had the great opportunity to rescue 300 princesses (prostitutes) off the streets. We call this particular ministry "Out of Darkness." The men and women who staff this ministry (both the employees and the volunteers) are an incredible bunch of people.

At a staff training, I was honored to share about how the Gospel of the Kingdom should be woven into the tapestry of our lives, including our encounters with every person God brings into our lives. Right before I began the training session, I learned that the group included some ladies who had just been rescued out of prostitution. I was so honored they were there.

As I was sharing the Gospel of the Kingdom, these ladies' eyes were locked on me—it seemed they were soaking up every word. At the end of the message, the Lord prompted my heart to explain to these ladies that their lifestyle was less offensive to God than my past lifestyle. If you were to compare my life with theirs, most people would say that mine looked far better according to worldly standards, even angelic in comparison. But from a kingdom view, my life was far worse.

Why would my life—full of church, Bible college, outreach, and moving in the power of God—be worse from a Kingdom view than a woman in prostitution? Since we now know that "the sin" is the desire to be our own god/king and that we do not need to repent merely for all the fruit (sins) we have on our tree (our lives), but must repent for our treason (the sin), it opens our eyes to God's concept of justice instead of man's.

Let's start with the ladies. They had been living boldly in the power and influence of "the sin." That is not good. But they never claimed to be doing a great job of following God or His ways.

On the other hand, I was not only living the partial conversation, I was preaching it. I was preaching true facts without actually having (or preaching) the Truth. Telling people to repent for what they had done, receive what He has done, try to follow Him with the help of the Holy Spirit, and you will be saved. By living and preaching a partial conversation, I was unintentionally telling people that God had come to bail them out of their debts (sins) without ever telling them that they needed to repent for their desire for their kingdom (the sin).

In other words, I only told people to repent of what they did. I failed to tell them to repent of their kingdom, like Jesus said we need to do. Matthew 4:17. I was basically telling people they could have God and keep their kingdom. In essence, I ignorantly counseled people that God would assist them in becoming a better king.

I gave them Lordship messages but I never gave them the Kingdom message. Having a Lord over you is not the same as having a kingdom in, over, and around you. Lordship does not require one to love what the Lord loves and hate what He hates. It just requires you to submit. Because I did not have the whole message but only the parts we all like to hear, I was telling people that they could still sit on the throne and just give God a spot. I like the term "half-cheeking it." We half-cheek it when we give the Lord a part of our throne, while keeping a part for ourselves.

We can see an analogy to enjoying God's power without accepting His kingdom in the military relationship between the United States and Canada. The United States shares a border with Canada. Canada doesn't have or need a big military force because it is next to the world's greatest military. Canada knows that if it's invaded, it can call America to help it out. But just because Canada loves that protection doesn't mean it wants to become the 51st state. It wants to be Canada. I'm not criticizing them for that—it's just a fact. Canada enjoys America's power, but doesn't want to lose its culture, economy, or way of doing things by joining the United States.

When I preached a partial-gospel message, people loved hearing they could have their debt paid and that the super power of heaven would deliver them if they were attacked. This message allowed the listener to still be them, loving what they loved and hating what they hated—whether or not their loves and hates lined up with God's. The culture of our own kingdom is to give God access to some aspects of our lives, while retaining complete control over other aspects, all with the goal of reaping the maximum benefit for us (including salvation).

I was committing treason in the name of Christ and telling others that they could do the same. I'm not alone. A lot of people have done the same, (whether through their personal lives, testimonies, sermons, books, etc.), spreading the partial gospel that one can be saved simply by repenting for the things they've done and believing that Jesus died on the cross and rose again. That message ultimately tells people they can be bailed out of their debts (sins) without the need to repent of *the* sin—the desire to be king.

A message that bails you out but does not take you out is a message that uses God's word to promote treason instead of delivering people. That's what I did as a young pastor. I'll ask you the same question I asked those ladies rescued from prostitution. Who is worse: (1) the woman who bluntly chooses to live outside God's Kingdom by living for her own; or (2) me, who told people essentially that salvation is a bailout, teaching people who showed up at church seeking God that they could remain sitting on the throne of their hearts? Whose treason is worse?

b)   Deception is no excuse

Maybe some of us have been deceived into thinking that we can serve God while sitting on our throne. Or, if we're honest, maybe we loved the idea of being our own king so much that we only listened to the part of the songs, small-group discussions, or sermons that didn't threaten our desire to have a Savior without accepting a King. But even if there's a whole church united in agreement that we can receive salvation while being of our own kingdoms, that doesn't make it so. Jesus prayed that we would have unity, but that unity must be in Christ, not against Christ.

Think of the tower of Babel. God told Noah and his sons to multiply and fill the earth (Gen. 9:1), but instead the people decided to build a city and a tower with its top in the heavens. Genesis 11:4. Like many today, our ancestors wanted to get to heaven on their own terms. The people strove for unity, but instead of uniting to fill the earth with the fame of the Lord, they united in saying, "let us make a name for ourselves, lest we be scattered abroad over the face of the whole earth." Gen. 11:4. That was unity in rebellion, not unity in obedience to the King.

So even if we have been deceived into thinking we can have Jesus while remaining in our own kingdom, it won't excuse our treason any more than it did Eve's. If Eve's example isn't enough, the Old Testament describes the entire kingdom of Israel following the trail of deception during the days of Isaiah the prophet. In those days, Israel's prophets were leading the people astray, blessing those who took care of them financially and cursing those who didn't. Micah 3:5.

Isaiah warned Israel that its lying prophets would be destroyed. But not only would the prophets be destroyed, so would all those who followed them. Isaiah 9:13-16. He said, "The Lord will have no joy in their young men, nor have mercy on their fatherless and widows." Isaiah 9:17. Like Eve, the Israelites' journey began in deception, but the destination was the same as those who, like Adam, embraced *the* sin with their eyes open. They became evildoers, and suffered the consequences. Isaiah 9:17.

Paul explains it even more starkly in 2 Thessalonians. He warns that in the last days, the antichrist (that is, the one who is against—"anti"—our King and High Priest) will come, by authority of Satan, "with all wicked deception for those who are perishing, because they refused to love the truth and so be saved." 2 Thessalonians 2:9-10. Look at why Paul says the people will be deceived. It isn't because the Truth wasn't available to them. It's because they didn't want it. When we succumb to deception, it is because we didn't love the Truth—we liked the sound of the deception better.

c)   Who do you say you are?

Imagine one of those prostitutes I mentioned above. Picture her being dragged into a king's courtroom to stand before him for judgment. You and I are the jury. She doesn't look like what you expected. In fact, she doesn't look that different from you. Or, at least she wouldn't if it weren't for those filthy rags she's wearing. Where have they been keeping her? She looks scared, standing before the king.

The prosecutor stands at the right side of the prostitute, accusing her of a long list of crimes. She has plenty of victims. But the prosecutor is crafty—he wants to use his time on the crimes most likely to bring a conviction. This isn't just any prostitute. He accuses her of stealing money and frittering it away on selfish luxuries; not just stealing from anyone, but from the king's own treasury. He accuses her of abusing children, and not just any children, but the king's own children. He accuses her of every sexual immorality known to man, and not just with anyone, but drawing the king's own servants into adultery.

But that's not all. The prosecutor saves the most egregious crime for last. He accuses her of conspiring against the king himself, of plotting to dethrone the king. He accuses her of treason. And he has proof.

The prosecutor queues up a video, showing a scene from the king's own throne room. While the king traveled in a distant land, we see the prostitute sneaking into the throne room and seating herself on the king's throne. We watch as she relishes in her treason, holding drunken orgies with the men who join in her sexual immoralities. She sits as a queen, dressed in purple and scarlet, adorned with gold and jewels and pearls—the wages of her sin. We listen as she confidently announces from the comfort of the king's throne, "I am, and there is no one besides me."

As the video ends, the prosecutor rests. The king turns to the prostitute. You expect to see fury in his eyes, but you see more than that—you see that his heart is crushed by what he saw on the video.

How will the prostitute respond? At her side lays a sheaf of papers setting out the defense she had always planned to provide if caught. Her defense showed she wasn't all bad. It talked about the good things she had done while seated on the king's throne. She had used the authority she had seized to feed some homeless people in the king's territory. She made time to drive her kids hundreds of miles for baseball and soccer games. She even volunteered for her church's middle-school youth group—truly a sacrifice!

But now, faced with her crimes while standing before the king, her defenses go unspoken. She comes to the realization that merely doing some good things with her stolen authority didn't make her good. In fact, she sees that she had been in slavery to *the* sin, her desire to be queen.

She who was shameless now stands ashamed. She who spoke words smoother than oil to seduce men into adultery and treason now stands speechless. She who clothed herself in fine linen and silk now stands in filthy garments. She has no defense. The verdict is guilty. The judge confirms her guilt and says the penalty of her crimes, her treason, is death. The guards lock her in their arms to lead her to the torturers who will carry out the execution.

Let's shift the focus for a moment. Instead of looking outwardly, look inwardly. In accepting Jesus as King and His Kingdom, we all had to come to terms with something. We had to own up to who we really are. We weren't the jury. The reason the prostitute didn't look that different from us is because she was us. Before we accepted Christ as King, we were the prostitute who would be queen. The prostitute who would say, "I am, and there is no one besides me" (Isaiah 47:7), even when the Lord says, "I am . . . and there is no other." Isaiah 45:6.

Sometimes, people think they don't have a good enough testimony. Like, "I was raised in the church. Sure, I broke a few rules here and there, but I never did anything *really* bad." We look at the drug-dealer-turned-fiery-gospel-preacher and envy his testimony. If that's ever been you, congratulations! You were a treasonous harlot. We all were.

Why does the "prostitute" label apply to everyone outside of Christ? We have all prostituted ourselves to idols. We have trusted in something or someone other than the Lord God, the Creator of heavens and earth. We offered our money, our attention, our heart to them, trusting in them to give us the desires of our hearts—even though they could never give us the peace our hearts longed for.

Instead of receiving the prostitute's wages, we offered ourselves for free, showering our idols with the devotion that was meant for our Creator. What prostitute gives gifts to her lovers rather than the other way around? We did. *See* Ezekiel 16:33-34. That's reality. We have to own that. If we do, something amazing awaits us.

d)   It is finished: the prostitute's redemption

Remember that God sees everything. We stand stripped before Him, the shame of our nakedness exposed to His eyes. The fruits of our spiritual immorality poured out upon us. Yet He still wanted us. "God demonstrates His own love toward us, in that while we were still sinners, Christ died for us." Romans 5:8.

As we, the condemned prostitute, wait for our sentence to be carried out, the King calls, "Remove the filthy garments from her and clothe her with pure garments!" The King's servants are confused—the death sentence must be carried out. Their King is a just King. Treason does not go unpunished. Then they gasp as understanding dawns over them. The King calls on His Son to present Himself to the torturers. The Son goes willingly.

They do their job without mercy. They beat the Son with a whip imbedded with metal that rips His skin. They strip Him of His clothes and dress Him in royal finery, not to restore Him to His throne, but to mock Him. They press a crown of thorns upon His head. They spit upon Him. They beat Him with a wooden rod. Then they nail Him to a wooden cross and let Him hang until He dies. Even then, they don't let Him die in peace, but use His dying hours for entertainment, giving Him wine contaminated with gall, mocking Him, and speculating on whether the prophet Elijah would show up to save Him. And finally, "He said, 'It is finished!' And bowing His head, He gave up His spirit." John 19:30.

When Jesus said, "It is finished," He meant it. We who believe in Him are forgiven. "In Him we have redemption through His blood, the forgiveness of sins, according to the riches of His grace." Ephesians 1:7. What does that mean? Not only are we forgiven, but purity is restored. Those who believe "have washed their robes and made them white in the blood of the Lamb." Revelation 7:14. The blood of Jesus "cleanses us from all sin." 1 John 1:7.

What more could we ask than the forgiveness of our treason? We couldn't ask for anything, but He offers still more. Much more. In fact, "No eye has seen, no ear has heard, and no mind has imagined what God has prepared for those who love Him." 1 Corinthians 2:9 (NLT).

When the King asked His Son to step off His throne to take the death penalty for the shameless prostitute, He did more than purchase her forgiveness. He says to those who throw open the gates of their hearts, "You have been redeemed. You who hope in Me are pure." He purchased her from slavery. She was bought with a price. He designated her for marriage to His Son. And he dealt with Her as a daughter. See Exodus 21:9.

To the prostitute who said in her heart, "I am a queen," but now repents of such a position and desire, the Father says, "You are my daughter. You are she who was lost and now is found. She who was dead and now is alive." See Luke

15:22-24. To her, He says, "Take off those filthy rags and put on the robe of many colors worn by my virgin daughter to await the day of your wedding." See Zechariah 3:4; Psalm 45:13-15.[17]

And what does the Son, the Bridegroom, say to His bride (the church)? He says, "You are glorious; You are altogether beautiful, My love; there is no flaw in you." See Ephesians 5:27; Song of Solomon 4:7. He says, "I desire that you would be with me where I am, that you may behold My glory." See John 17:24.

The bride is the church, and believers individually are the members of her body—His body. In the Song of Solomon, the bridegroom says to the bride, "Behold, you are beautiful, my love." Song of Solomon 4:1. But he doesn't stop there. He goes on to recount the beauty He sees in her individual members: her eyes, her hair, her teeth, her lips, her cheeks, her neck, her breasts, her thighs, her belly, her navel, her nose, her head, her stature? Song of Solomon 4, 7. Can we understand what He's saying: "You are beautiful, my church, my bride. And so is each and every one of your members."

"As the bridegroom rejoices over the bride, so shall your God rejoice over you." Isaiah 62:5 (ESV). "The LORD your God is living among you. . . . He will take delight in you with gladness. With his love, he will calm all your fears. He will rejoice over you with joyful songs." Zephaniah 3:17 (NLT).[18]

When we hear the song of Jesus rejoicing over us, we will

---

[17] The story of the prostitute being tried for her crimes before the King draws on several Bible passages, including Zechariah 3, John 8, Isaiah 45 and 47, Luke 22, John 19, Psalm 45, Ephesians 5, and Revelation 19. Additional inspiration for this section came from *The Harlot*, a song by Misty Edwards that just might change your life.

[18] If you have trouble imagining Jesus rejoicing over you in song, try listening to Misty Edwards' song, *Do You Know the Way You Move Me*.

understand the words of the old hymn, "Joyful, joyful we adore thee, God of glory, Lord of love. Hearts unfold like flowers before thee, opening to the sun above. Melt the clouds of sin and sadness, drive the doubt away. Giver of immortal gladness, fill us with the light of day!"[19]

2.   Who is the One who would endure the cross?

What person would do all this for a treasonous prostitute? What judge? What president? What king would do such an act? Only one. The King of kings! The Great I AM! The Alpha and Omega! Jesus Christ would do such a thing. He did such an act.

We sometimes refer to Jesus' work, in shorthand, as "the cross." But it's not really the cross that has the power. After all, the Roman Empire crucified many people. In 71 B.C., the Romans "lined the road from Capua to Rome with 6,000 crucified rebels on 6,000 crosses."[20] In Jerusalem, Rome crucified thousands of Jews before and after Jesus—as many as 500 a day in the months leading up to the destruction of Jerusalem in 70 A.D.[21] Many people died horrible deaths on the cross. But only one of them died for *the* sin in accordance with the Scriptures.

So it's not so much about the cross, but the One who went to the cross. When we consider who that One is, the power of the cross will hit us so much harder. Who is that One? Paul says it so well in Colossians 1:15-18. Jesus is:

---

[19] Henry J. Van Dyke, "The Hymn of Joy," *Book of Poems*, Third Ed., 1911.
[20] "A Tomb in Jerusalem Reveals the History of Crucifixion and Roman Crucifixion Methods," Bible Archaeology Society, July 22, 2011, accessed Nov. 16, 2016, http://www.biblicalarchaeology.org/daily/biblical-topics/crucifixion/a-tomb-in-jerusalem-reveals-the-history-of-crucifixion-and-roman-crucifixion-methods/.
[21] Ibid.

- The image of the invisible God;

- The firstborn over all creation;

- Before all things, and in Him all things consist (that is, hold together);

- By Him all things were created that are in heaven and that are on earth, visible and invisible, whether thrones or dominions or principalities or powers—all things were created through Him and for Him;

- The head of the body, the church;

- He is the beginning, the firstborn from the dead.

And look how Paul wraps it up: "that in all things He may have the preeminence." Colossians 1:15-18. Who has preeminence? The King. The King of kings, the Lord of lords. This is the Christ who "died for our sins . . . [and] rose again the third day according to the Scriptures." 1 Corinthians 15:3-4. Can you wait until the day comes when Isaiah's prophecy is fulfilled, and our "eyes will see the King in His beauty"? Isaiah 33:17.

The difficult concept to understand is that Jesus was hung on a cross for treason—for declaring Himself king of the Jews. That's difficult to understand because Jesus never committed treason—He is the King of kings, so He cannot commit treason against Himself. The ones guilty of treason are you, me, and the mob who demanded Jesus' crucifixion!

The Roman governor Pontius Pilate said he found no guilt in Jesus, but the Jewish religious leaders demanded His crucifixion, saying, "We have no king but Caesar!" John 18:15. Fearing man (the emperor), Pilate joined with the people of Israel against the Lord's anointed, turning Jesus over for crucifixion. Acts 4:27. The people mocked Jesus as though He were a fake king. They beat, spit upon, and brutalized Him, trying to drive home the point that he was not king over them. Jesus was punished for treason by the ones who thought they were justified by their earthly authority—for the Jews, their physical descent from Abraham, and for the Romans, their earthly kingdom.

In reality, both Jews and Gentiles were lawless—they were the ones who committed treason. Those who put Jesus to death were the ones who should have been put to death. But instead of the King of kings judging them by the law to execute them for treason, He poured out mercy and paid the price for their treason, our treason. Mercy triumphs over judgment. James 2:13. What king would pay the price for his people committing treason, knowing most would never repent, many would want His power and salvation, and only a few would repent of their treason and love Him and His ways? Only the true King. The One and only!

3.   He's the subject, we're the object—it's a lot better that way

Sometimes, people are disappointed when they find out that the Gospel isn't about them. That it's actually about the Kingdom—the King and His culture. But as we get to know King Jesus, we come to understand that it's so much better this way. Think about our lives when we try to be the subject of our conversation, when we try to make it all about us. Does that end well? I know it didn't for me.

Let's let Him be the subject of the conversation. It's incredible to believe that Jesus would do this for us—a bunch of traitors. It's even more intense when you consider that Jesus did this knowing that most would never care, that others would say thank you and try to take Him for all that He has, and that only a few would fall in love with Him and

His culture.

Contemplate the King of kings, who has no need for anything or anyone. Imagine Him lowering Himself by taking on the form of humanity, by actually being born of a woman. And, finally, being tortured and murdered by His own creation who themselves had committed treason and led others into treason. Why did He do this, even while we were still sinners? Romans 5:8.

Scripture gives us the answer. It tells us why Jesus agreed to pay that terrible price, why He "endured the cross," even though he "despis[ed] the shame": He did it "for the joy that we set before Him." Hebrews 12:2. For we who believe!

I don't know how the conversation went when the Father and the Son talked about the price to be paid for God's elect, but I imagine there was a question posed from Son to Father: "My Father, where is the lamb for an offering." See Genesis 22:7. And the response: "God will provide for himself the lamb for an offering." See Genesis 22:8. And we know the response of the Son: "Not My will, but Yours, be done." Luke 22:42. Hallelujah! Truly, "Salvation belongs to our God who sits on the throne, and to the Lamb!" Revelation 7:10.

It would be easy to look at the Scriptures saying that the saints were chosen before the foundation of the world and buy into the idea that we believers are the subject of the conversation. We're not. God is the subject. But take heart, for we are the object of the conversation! We are the object of His love. How incredible is that?

E.   The Invitation

If you're realizing that you've been in vain conversation with God, thinking you can receive the benefits of salvation without forsaking your own kingdom, I bring you Good News—the Gospel.

What is the Gospel? It's not about me (or you). Jesus told us what the Gospel is—He said it's the "gospel of the kingdom." Matthew 24:14. What is the Kingdom? The King and His culture. Heaven is invading earth. The Kingdom is upon you. Matthew 12:28. The poor in spirit welcome it—they give glory and worship to Him who made heaven and earth. Revelation 14:6.

The Kingdom of Heaven is at hand. Repent of sitting on His throne. Seek the Kingdom of God and His righteousness. Seek the King and His culture. Love what He loves and hate what He hates. Count the cost, understanding that you must forsake everything—past, present, and future. If you seek the Kingdom, counting the cost, the price of your treason has been paid by the One who was victimized by your treason. And His Kingdom will enter you and you will enter His Kingdom.

Have you ever thrown open the gates of your heart, singing, "Hosanna—blessed is He who comes in the name of the Lord," as the King takes your throne? Maybe you did it once, but have since tried to re-take the throne of your life from Him. If so, I encourage you to stop living a vain conversation. Repent of your desire to be your own king, cast your crown before Jesus, and usher Him who died and rose again onto the throne of your heart.

Let today be the day of salvation! The king is dead; long live the King!

Made in the USA
Lexington, KY
04 August 2017